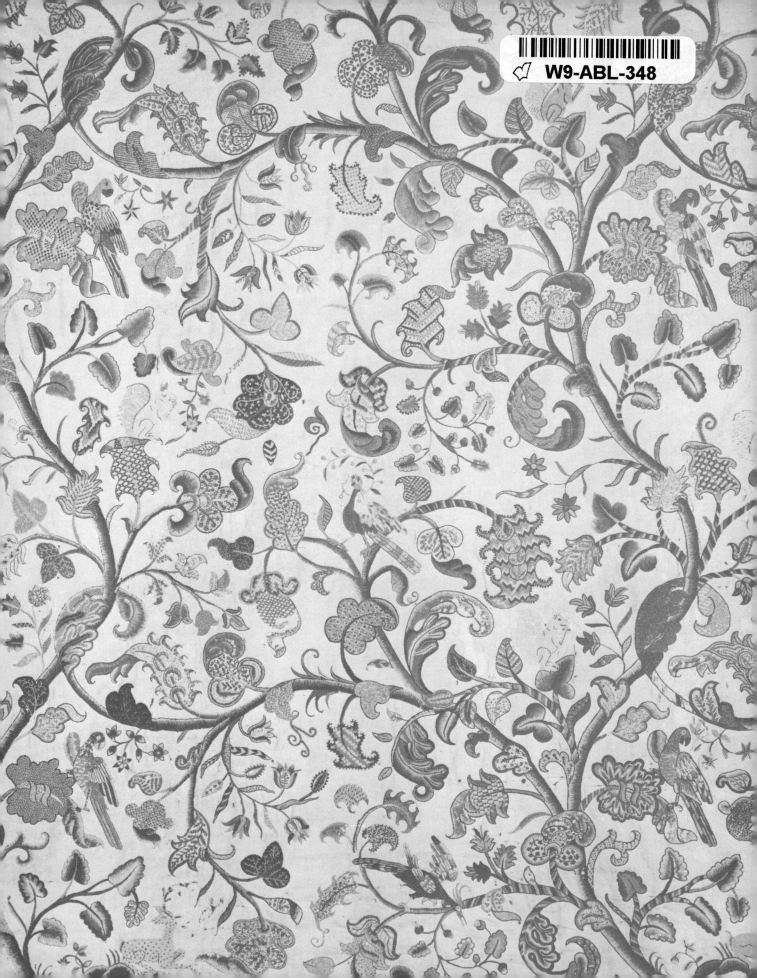

Pleasures of Crewel

THE *Betty Crocker* HOME LIBRARY

Pleasures of
Crewel

A BOOK OF ELEMENTARY TO ELEGANT STITCHES
AND NEW EMBROIDERY DESIGNS

by Jo Springer

UNIVERSAL PUBLISHING INC. UPd NEW YORK

DISTRIBUTED BY CHARLES SCRIBNER'S SONS

Acknowledgments
Stitch Drawings by Marta Cone
Diagrams by Solweig Hedin
Photographs by Frank Stork

This book published simultaneously
in the United States of America and Canada—
Copyright under the Berne Convention.

Library of Congress Catalog Card Number 70-177368

Betty Crocker is a trademark of General Mills, Inc.,
which is licensed for use to
Universal Publishing and Distributing Corporation.
Printed in the United States of America

Contents

Dear Friend,

How can the fascination of crewel embroidery best be explained? As a nostalgic reminder of our old-world heritage? Or as an exciting venture into contemporary, creative handcraft? Actually, it is both of these and more. At once stimulating and relaxing, challenging and satisfying, crewel embroidery is a personal expression both timely and timeless in its appeal.

The "pleasures" of this book are intended for needleworkers new *and* experienced. Whether used as primer, refresher course or for pure inspiration, you should find guidance and encouragement in these pages. The author is one of the country's foremost needle-workers: editor, teacher, writer and member of the prestigious Embroiderers' Guild of America. Her stitches and projects cover the broadest range, from simple to complex. But beyond these, as your skills and interest develop, we hope you will be tempted to adapt and experiment on your own. A promise: the rewards will be considerable. In embroidering for yourself or for others you will find joy in creating handwork that reflects your talent, patience and imagination.

An embroidery needle makes the tiniest of holes. Yet is it big enough to open up the "whole" enchanting world of embroidery—providing beautiful and cherished heirlooms for all your tomorrows.

Betty Crocker

1. The Story of Crewel Embroidery

If all the embroidery stitches made since the beginning of time were laid end to end, they would form a decorative ribbon to the moon, perhaps even to the far reaches of our galaxy. What is it about a little steel needle and a length of colored yarn that creates in people the urge to transform that yarn into a design of stitches on any piece of fabric that comes to hand? How did it all begin? Where is it leading us? We'll explore some of these questions as our story unfolds. But first, what is crewel?

Crewel is just one form of embroidery. The differentiating factor (and it isn't a hard and fast rule) is that crewel embroidery is worked with wool. The word "crewel" derives from the word "clew," meaning a ball of yarn or worsted thread. In old manuscripts crewel was often spelled "crule" or "cruell," but the very fact that it was mentioned in manuscripts, household inventories, even in last wills and testaments indicates that crewel embroidery had a distinguished place in the lives of our forebears.

Perhaps a quick look into the history of crewel will invest it with the romance that it deserves and at the same time will divest it of the mystery that surrounds it. Unfortunately, recorded history is less

Endleaves: Museum examples of fine crewel act as inspiration to today's needleworkers. This English curtain of the early eighteenth century shows many typical Jacobean elements. *Courtesy of Royal Ontario Museum, Toronto, Canada.*

1

thorough in describing the creative aspects of life than it is about its destructive side. Wars are always better documented than the arts. Although embroidery has been a common art for hundreds of years, only a few outstanding pieces have remained to delight us.

The average housewife may have glowed in the ownership of a pretty petticoat or the hard-working farmer may have been proud of his embroidered shirt. But since they had to wear them until they fell in shreds, there is no record of the needlework of the ordinary people of earlier times. Only a rich and formal household kept an inventory of its possessions. Those who lived in manor houses and castles handed down their embroideries so that we can see them now three and four hundred years later. Remember, however, that the examples in museums and national shrines both here and in Europe are only the tip of the iceberg. A great mass of embroidery was used and enjoyed, then disappeared. Yet it, too, had its effect on our stitchery today.

Where crewel began is lost in the mists of time. Perhaps it arose from man's basic need for beauty and self-adornment. As embroiderers we owe a great deal to the first caveman who picked up a bright blue feather and stuck it in the animal skin he was wearing.

We do know that crewel was being worked a thousand years ago. The most famous example is the Bayeux tapestry. This is not a true woven tapestry at all but an embroidered wall hanging worked in crewel stitches on linen. It is a remarkable work some 20 inches high by an astounding 230 feet long. In graphic form it tells the story of the Norman Conquest of England. It can be viewed in Bayeux, France, today although it was finished about nine hundred years ago by Queen Mathilda (wife of William the Conquerer) or by women working under her direction. Even with the aid of six neighbors, can you imagine working 230 feet of embroidery?

Crewel embroidery flourished during the Middle Ages both on the Continent and in England. Those years from A.D. 400 to 1400 weren't necessarily the Dark Ages in terms of embroidery. But the work was not a source of personal pleasure, as far as we know, since it was institutionalized and was generally carried on in convents and abbeys where it was executed for church use. One wonders, however, what embroideries must have decorated the lives of the common people—serf, peasant and tradesman alike. Did they stitch in the symbols which were a holdover from the earlier tribal days? Did they use these embroideries in their rituals—dancing, marriages, births? We'll never know.

Like so many of the arts, embroidery languished for a time and it was not until the sixteenth and seventeenth centuries in England that the revival of embroidery produced the style that we think of as typical of crewel. Strangely enough a little thing like a needle was the cause of it all. There seems to be a direct relationship between the early manufacturing of steel needles in England and the renaissance of crewel embroidery. No doubt steel needles manufactured in Germany for over one hundred and fifty years had found their way to England, but the larger supply of less expensive needles must have had a great deal to do with the burgeoning of crewel in this era.

A glimpse into Elizabethan England in the late 1500's, and at the rest of the world in the period immediately following Elizabeth's time, may give us some insight into what produced such beautiful embroideries. It was a period of much religious and political turmoil. In England, Henry VIII left a legacy of disunity, intrigue and scandal. But in the midst of this violence were great internal growth and development as well as foreign exploration, trade and expansion. Many people of this era were less interested in matters of the spirit than those of the flesh. One French queen had a gown embroidered with 32,000 pearls and 3,000 diamonds—all of them real. Society became highly materialistic and beautiful objects produced locally or brought with great hardship from distant lands were highly prized. Ornate clothing as well as luxurious home furnishings were cherished. Embroideries fell into this last category.

Hangings led all other items in importance. We can make some educated guesses about this. First, since hangings were large and important in themselves, they were not discarded as lightly as smaller objects might have been; thus they have remained to find their way into museums and private collections. Second, basic human comfort was a factor. In unheated drafty houses, stone castles and wooden structures alike, anything that added to the warmth or cheer of the house was treasured. Wall hangings and bed hangings cut down on the ever-present drafts in the chill interiors. As a result, hangings are among the most common relics of the past.

Nevertheless, many other items were embroidered. Carpets for tables and (more rarely) for floors, seats for chairs, stools and benches, bedspreads—as wide a variety of household items as are currently embroidered were favorite objects to be embellished with stitchery. Just as today's needleworker uses her bits and pieces of fabric and yarn to make any number of small items, so did the Elizabethan needleworker make pincushions, workbags, book covers, and sachets. Of course, personal decoration was not neglected. Petticoat borders, bodices, hoods, even entire garments were usually ornate and trimmed with a wealth of embroidery. Nor was this form of decoration limited to women's clothing. The men also enjoyed richly ornamented garments.

This embroidery was rarely crewel as we know it. The stitchery was usually carried out in silk threads (occasionally combined with wool) on a canvas-type cloth of linen or other fibers. Garments, however, were made of a variety of fabrics—silk, wool, linen, velvet, and so on. The embroidery was developed with a wide variety of stitches, all of them familiar to needleworkers today. The color selection was as wide as that of the stitches. Pastels as well as bright colors were used in a naturalistic manner. The favorite symbols and devices for designs were objects from nature—both the familiar and the exotic. Garden flowers such as daffodils and lilies and such fruits as apples and pears were shown along with never-seen tropical blossoms, pomegranates and pineapples. The fauna of England as well as the animals of more distant lands were all shown in embroidery. No insect was too insignificant to be celebrated on someone's embroidered design.

Embroidery was definitely not a peasant art in Elizabethan times. And, although there was a growing middle class, the art of embroidery extended only part way into this group. The work was carried on at court and in the highest social circles. Actually, Queen Elizabeth herself was a well-known embroideress and did more to

IN MAGNO : NAVIGIO :

A small segment of the Bayeux Tapestry, one of the national treasures of France. *Courtesy of French Cultural Services.*

formalize embroidery than did any other reigning monarch. In 1561 she granted a charter to the Broderers' Company, more formally known as the "Keepers and Wardens and Society of the Art and Mistery of the Broderers of the City of London." This was a guild of craftsmen (note that they were men) who were responsible for some of the great works executed in this Age of Embroidery. It would be interesting to know how the skills were transferred from the great ladies of the court who embroidered for pleasure to these craftsmen who embroidered for a living. And it was not an easy way to earn a living! Each piece they executed had to be presented at the Guild Hall for inspection and the seal of approval of the Guild. If the work did not meet the exacting standards, it was cut up and burned.

During this century many of the elements of crewel embroidery took on their modern form. The detached flower, curling stems, isolated bird and animal forms all took shape in sixteenth-century needlework. Then early in the seventeenth century, James I took the

throne in England. In the formal Latin parlance of the day he was known as *Jacobus Brittaniae Rex*. From this comes the term "Jacobean." In fact, crewel is so tied up with the period that it is often called Jacobean embroidery. In the mid-to-late seventeenth century (actually after the death of James I) the "typical" forms of crewel were crystallized. The well-known Tree of Life design rising from curving mounds or hillocks became popular. Its oversize leaves, curvaceous blossoms and crowded details were standards for crewel of the period. Many Oriental influences are evident. These contained both Indian and Chinese elements. Some interesting speculation and studies have been made about the origins of the Oriental influence. For example, the large *palampores*, or painted hangings, that were popular imports from India were believed to be the source of some crewel designs.

Actually, the influence was probably not that direct. English embroideries were possibly influenced first by Chinese imports. Then the Indians, when they made their painted wall hangings, catered to British taste by following the Chinese-inspired English embroideries. When the Indian hangings finally came to England, they, in turn, influenced later British embroideries. This is a good example of the far-reaching effects of world trade!

The days of Oliver Cromwell had a subduing influence on English crewel in the 1650's, but with the Restoration of the monarchy in 1660 came an upsurge of interest in embroidery once again, no doubt because of a revival of interest in dress and other worldly pleasures after the somber Puritan years. In fact, toward the end of the seventeenth century embroidery was particularly admired since Queen Mary, wife of William of Orange, was an ardent embroideress. In the last decade of the century, however, crewel fell out of favor, to be replaced by silk embroideries. And there was little interest in crewel work throughout the eighteenth century.

Across the seas in the Colonies before the Revolutionary War, a bit of crewel was carefully brought in sea chests from the Old

This antique English curtain dated 1696, now in Canada, is one of the oldest pieces of crewel embroidery in the Western hemisphere. *Courtesy of Royal Ontario Museum, Toronto, Canada.*

World. Early settlers had more serious activities to fill their busy days, however. Farming, spinning and weaving, sewing, candle and soap making were only a few of their chores. Handwork grew out of need for the objects it produced, many from scrap materials; therefore rug making and patchwork were the needlecrafts of the Colonies rather than embroidery. Only a few dedicated embroiderers kept the art of crewel alive.

A fascinating period in American history developed at this time even though the art wasn't widespread. We call it the "blue and white" era because the embroidery was worked mainly in those two colors. And for a very good reason! Those Colonial dames had to spin and weave their own flax to produce their background fabrics. Then they had to card, spin and dye their own embroidery yarns. Since commercial dyes were seldom available, they grew their own indigo plants for the blue color they loved. The white came, of course, from the natural color of the wool. With all the labor involved in preparing for embroidery, is it any wonder they didn't have a wider range of colors?

The eighteenth century brought changes, however. The young country now had larger towns where women had more leisure and a chance to exchange patterns and ideas with neighbors. Crewel embroidery really took hold for the first time. The ever-popular bed hangings and covers, garments such as petticoat hems and aprons and many small items were cherished products delicately embellished with wool stitchery. Adaptations of English patterns were popular, but American needleworkers soon started to choose their own colors and space the units of the designs in their own way, giving their work a distinctly American flavor.

It is well known that little girls of six and eight did elaborate embroidered samplers. By the time these youngsters reached their mid-teens, they were experienced needlewomen and well-brought-up young ladies began embroidering their wedding dresses. What more natural outlet for a romantic young lady than to work a gown for that day of days? Worked in colored wools on linen, these wedding dresses are one of the high points in American crewel history.

About 1800 crewel once again began to be replaced in England and in the United States by a number of other forms of needlework. It was not until the last quarter of the century that Victorian ladies rediscovered crewel. The establishment of schools of needlework in London and New York gave the revival impetus. In this era an amazing amount of all types of needlework—lace making, beadwork, crocheting, and the like—was produced in an endless stream by ardent needlewomen. At the same time the commercial market for needlework was filled with handmade items made in convents, small factories and even in the home in undeveloped parts of the world.

With the new century all that was laid aside. The war in 1914, the emancipation of women with its accompanying interest in public affairs, sports, community activities and jobs provided less and less time for the hand arts. World War II revived a few practical needlecrafts such as sewing and knitting, but television soon absorbed much of the free time of most people. Then suddenly, in mid-twentieth century, a rapid about-face took place. People found themselves with increased leisure—and increased pressures from the world around them. These two factors practically cry out for the relaxing effects of doing handwork. What more natural result than another revival of crewel with all the deep personal satisfaction it brings?

The latest revival has inspired a rapid expansion of the art of crewel. Many embroiderers are experimenting with new materials and techniques as well as original designs. Since by definition the use of embroidery materials other than wool (for example, gold and silver, silk, linen and even cotton threads, jewels and feathers) technically takes the work out of the crewel category, a new, all-inclusive name for these innovations—creative stitchery—has been added to the needleworker's vocabulary. At the same time, the traditionalists are rivaling the work of the great embroiderers of earlier times. These two mainstreams—traditional crewel and creative stitchery—are being subjected to a constant flow of fresh, new, and daring ideas in the areas of design and materials. The question is, where will this great embroidery revival lead? It is fun to try to guess.

Peacock Embroidery
by a student at
The Royal School of Needlework,
London, England

Chessmen Embroidery
by a student also at
The Royal School of Needlework

2. Tools and Materials

Now it is time to settle down to the kind of information that is basic for anyone who wants to try her hand at embroidery.

The first question is where to work. Although you can embroider stretched out under a tree in the garden or curled up in an easy chair or decide to carry your work with you wherever you go, the ideal spot is in a straight chair with low (or no) arms near a table that holds your supplies. Be sure that an excellent and glare-free light comes over your left shoulder (if you are right-handed).

EMBROIDERY TOOLS

Fortunately only a minimum of very inexpensive equipment is needed by even the most advanced needleworker, so buy the best and keep it separate from the family sewing supplies so that it is always in perfect condition for your own use.

Needles

Crewel (or embroidery) needles have sharp points, are of medium length and have long eyes which make them easier to thread. Sizes from #3 (larger) to #8 (smaller) are about right for most wool work. When embroidering on a loose mesh fabric such as burlap, or when working surface stitches such as Weaving Stitch or Spider

Web, use a tapestry needle which has a blunt point. Needles can be purchased in a package of assorted sizes. In any case, use a needle large enough to produce a hole that will accommodate your yarn but not so big that it will force open the fibers of your fabric. The eye of the needle should, of course, be large enough to enable you to thread it easily.

Keep your needles in a pincushion, a piece of flannel or a needle case. In fact, it is convenient to have a small bag or box in which to keep your thimble, needles and scissors no matter how you store your needlework.

Scissors

Any scissors will do, but it's rather nice to consider your embroidery so special that you have a pair of scissors just for that purpose. Embroidery scissors have short narrow blades with sharp points. The points must close perfectly so that they will snip threads properly. If your scissors do not come with a little sheath to protect you as well as the blades, make one out of a bit of felt or leather. A pair of regular dressmaker's scissors will also be necessary for some of your projects.

Thimbles

If you plan to be the sort of needleworker who does a few stitches and calls it a day, a thimble may not be necessary. But for serious embroidery a thimble is a real help and a protection. Try on several metal (not plastic) thimbles until you find one that just fits your middle finger. Although you will, hopefully, learn to embroider with both hands, a thimble is necessary only on your right hand.

Embroidery Hoops

A few types of crewel stitches can be worked in the hand, but a hoop or a frame on which to stretch the background fabric is a necessity for most neat, unpuckered embroidery. You are probably well acquainted with the simplest, least expensive type—the hand-held embroidery hoop. It is made up of two rings or ovals of wood or metal from 3" to 12" in diameter. The wood hoop with an adjustable thumbscrew is the recommended type. The large sizes are more adaptable to a variety of work than the smaller ones which require constant moving over a large work area and leave pressure rings on your fabric.

Here are a few easy steps to follow when you are ready to insert the fabric in the hoop. First, baste in a temporary hem all around your background fabric (on which the design has been transferred) so the constant handling won't fray the edges. Tighten the screw on your hoop so that the rings fit together well; then separate the two rings. Lay the fabric *over* the inner ring, centering the design. Lay the outer ring *over* the fabric and press the outer ring over the inner one part way down. Stop and adjust fabric by pulling it tightly all the way around. CAUTION: Do *not* pull on the bias of the fabric or your embroidery may be distorted. Pull fabric as tight as a drum so that each stitch makes a little *ping* when it goes through the fabric. Press down the outer ring (if it will go any farther) and tighten screw if there is any free play. You are now ready to embroider. (Remember to release the work from the hoop whenever you put it away, to prevent permanent hoop marks.)

As you work and it becomes necessary to move the hoop over already embroidered areas, protect the embroidery with tissue paper. Just lay a sheet over your fabric before applying the outer ring of

Basic embroidery frame and hoop for the beginner.

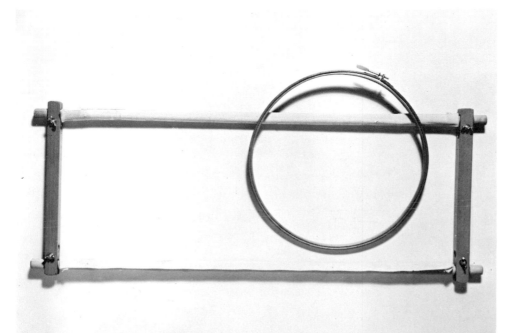

the hoop; then tear away the paper where you will do the next embroidery. This is also a useful method when working on fabrics such as silk that could be cut by the rubbing of the hoop.

Although the small hand-held hoop is desirable, since it fits neatly into a workbag, you will probably want to try other types as you become a more experienced needleworker. The hoop on a stand which sits on a table or in your lap is particularly convenient for the professional technique that will be discussed later. Some hoops can be clamped to a table. A hoop on a floor stand is also most useful for the serious needleworker. All of these hoops are adjustable in height and angle of work.

Embroidery Frames

Many people who do a great deal of needlework prefer frames to hoops since a good-size piece can be set up and need not be shifted until all the embroidery is completed. Commercial hand-held frames as well as floor frames are available. Both have some mechanism for rolling fabric at the top and bottom of the frame although the width of the frame is geared to fabric just 18", 24" or 36" wide.

Most frames come equipped with tapes attached to the rolling parts on which to sew the fabric. To use these frames, mark the center of the top tape. Baste a narrow hem in the top edge of your fabric and mark the center. Pin to center of top roller. Working from the center out, whip hem to tape. Fasten securely. Then repeat from center out to other edge. Repeat with bottom roller.

Frames vary in construction so adjust rollers or assemble frame so that work is taut. Sew a strip of heavy tape down each side of fabric. Lash these tapes to the sides of frame, tying them off at top and bottom so that they can be adjusted if the work loosens up.

If an embroidery frame is not available, you can use a sturdy discarded picture frame instead. Working on the back of the frame, thumbtack (or staple) the center of one side of the work in place; then the center of the opposite side. Continue tacking out to the corners, working first one side, then the other and placing tacks about 1" apart. Repeat process on the third and fourth sides.

Sometimes just the right size frame is not available. In that case,

Embroidery hoop in a stand for use on table or in lap. *Courtesy of the D. M. C. Corporation.*

Embroidery frame in a floor stand. *Courtesy of the D. M. C. Corporation.*

you might find it helpful to use artists' stretcher strips which are available in all sizes and can be purchased at any art supply store. Just hammer them together, making sure that the corners are square. Attach the fabric as for the picture frame.

To use a frame, rest the near side in your lap and the far side against a table.

FABRICS, EMBROIDERY WOOLS AND THREADS

Fabrics

Although traditional crewel was worked on twill linen or cotton and linen, feel free to choose your background fabrics from the great variety available in stores today. The choice is an exciting one limited only by taste and pocketbook. It is always wise, however, to choose sturdy, long-lasting fabric on which to spend your valuable time and effort. Linen of a medium weight and weave is a good choice as is smooth wool or the more loosely woven silks known as raw silk. Cotton in weaves such as homespun or hopsacking make excellent backgrounds. And don't overlook burlap, which is fine for modern wall hangings. You may even want to try using the stripes or checks of a fabric as a departure point for your stitchery. The little squares of a tablecloth check or stripes of a ticking make excellent patterns to follow. And for an exciting background for your stitchery see Accent Crewel, pages 96 and 97. Don't overlook many ready-made items as backgrounds for embroidery. Many young people are adding stitchery to their clothes. You might add a bright motif to the corner of a favorite head scarf, to the pocket of a shirt or the cuffs of a blouse. (For other suggestions, see page 158.)

If your heart is set on a particular fabric, try embroidering a sample on it before setting up your design. Will it take the design with one of the standard transfer methods? With the yarn and needle you have chosen to use, will the stitches pull through easily? Is the surface of the fabric sturdy enough so that it won't be abraded by the process of embroidery? Can it be washed or dry-cleaned? If the fabric is suitable for your project and can pass these tests, it will make a good background fabric.

Storing Fabrics

The ardent needleworker soon collects a pile of remnants and special fabrics she plans to use some day. With proper care these can be stored for years and will remain in good condition. If it is at all possible, fabrics—particularly linens—should be rolled rather than folded. Cardboard tubes, old broom handles, bamboo poles all make good bases for the roll. Wrap the roll in paper, label it and store it on a shelf or upright in a packing box in a closet.

If you keep your fabrics folded in a box or a drawer, refold in another way periodically so that the fabric will not permanently retain the fold marks.

Embroidery Wools and Threads

Crewel wool is a fine two-ply yarn that has a "crinkle" in its surface. In some needlework shops it can be purchased "loose" in short lengths by the ounce. Imported varieties are available in small skeins containing 20 yards. Cards containing 30 yards are also available. Note that the wool comes wound in one, two or three strands and is meant to be separated and used in any number of strands that you need. The colors are glorious and will give your creativity free rein.

Since crewel wool is available in only the best-stocked needlework shops and yarn departments, you may have to substitute whatever you have, or can buy, in the way of yarns. Knitting worsted, sports yarn, Shetland yarn, tapestry yarn—all can be used, depending on the weight needed. Just check to see that it will not fray in the embroidery process.

Although crewel is wool by definition, there's no need to inhibit yourself. A bit of silk floss (or rayon or even cotton) will add sparkle to an embroidery. Six-strand cotton is a well-known embroidery thread. Also try pearl cotton or knitting and crochet cottons. For couching a bold design you can even try certain stitches with twine or the thick synthetic tying yarns used for gift wraps. Many projects will benefit from the use of different weights and types of yarn all in the same piece. Much of the fun of working crewel is experimenting with materials. If you come across any of the Scandinavian linen threads, you'll find that they are lovely to work with. And don't forget what a bit of silver and gold can add to an embroidery.

It should be mentioned here that many creative needleworkers are including all sorts of unusual materials in their work these days. Modern hangings might have feathers worked into the stitchery, or beads, pearls, bits of beach glass or pebbles. Reeds, grasses or small dried branches have been used in some embroideries. When you start your own designing, you will begin to see the possibilities in the world around you.

Storing Yarn

Once you begin to collect yarns, you immediately have a storage problem. And no embroiderer can bear to throw away even the smallest scrap of yarn. Large skeins and balls can be stored in packing boxes, small skeins and cards of yarn can be lined up in a shoe box. But the ends and bits and pieces are the real problem. One of the most convenient storage aids is the empty core of a roll of paper towels. Wind the yarn or floss on the roll and tape the end. A different roll can be used for shades of one color or pieces of a particular type of yarn.

3. Planning Your Design

Needlework, like many activities, is done for the deep satisfaction it provides the doer, and the greatest satisfaction often comes from working on your own designs. Although a number of specific patterns follow in this book, they are meant to give you the experience and freedom to venture out on your own.

SOURCES OF DESIGN IDEAS

Unfortunately some needleworkers say they "can't draw a straight line" and never know the enjoyment of trying their hand at anything creative. Here's a little experiment to show you how artistic you really are. Tape a 15" square of fabric to your work table. Then take a good long length of heavy yarn and squiggle it around on the surface of the fabric. Let it overlap, circle back, spiral. Chances are that you now have a handsome modern design perfect for line embroidery. With a sharp pencil, mark in the lines of your squiggles. Now you are ready to cover the lines of your design with embroidery such as Couching or any of the line stitches you will learn later on. What a handsome pillow your embroidered square would make!

Here is an easy way to start an original design. First decide what you want to make—a pillow cover, a picture, or whatever you choose. Cut a piece of paper the right size and tape it to your work table.

Now take a juice glass and a water glass. Use them as patterns for circles which you can outline directly on your paper. Space them freely, overlapping a few circles. Using a dime and a quarter as patterns, scatter smaller circles in your design. You now have a bold design ready to transfer to your fabric (see instructions below). Try working the larger circles in any line stitch, the dime-size circles in solid Satin Stitch. But don't stop there. Work another row or two of line stitches inside the larger circles. And you thought you couldn't draw!

If you look around you, you can find hundreds of ideas for embroidery. As you begin to think more and more of your new hobby, you will find ideas in the birthday card in the morning mail, in the quaint pattern on a friend's antique plate, in the carving on the doors of a buffet or in the pages of a child's coloring book. Just remember that it is easier to adapt a flat design such as the one on your friend's plate or a design in a book than to translate a real bouquet of flowers into a working pattern.

Suppose you want to adapt a design from a handsome plate. Using a sheet of tracing paper, trace the main lines of the design. Enlarge or reduce the size as desired (see How to Enlarge and Reduce Designs, page 25). Now you are ready to transfer the pattern to your background fabric by the most appropriate method.

HOW TO TRANSFER DESIGNS

Carbon Paper Method

With masking tape fasten your background fabric in position right side up on a smooth firm surface. Then tape carbon paper in place right side (carbon side) down on your fabric. Use as many sheets of carbon paper as needed for the size of the design. Now tape design in place right side up. Be sure that there is plenty of fabric all around the edges of the design. With pencil or stylus go over all lines of design. Check to see if you are bearing down hard enough to transfer the lines.

Ordinary carbon paper often smudges when you are working the embroidery. Try to find the plastic, non-smudge type of carbon paper

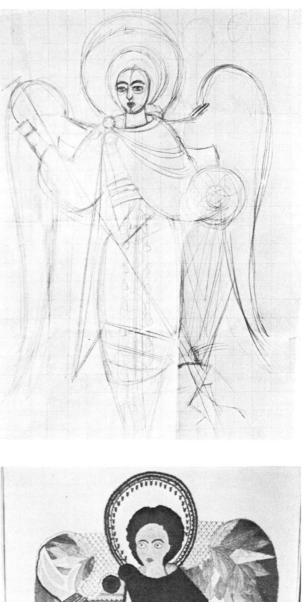

A reproduction of an icon
of St. Michael in Pisa, Italy,
with the rough sketch taken
from it for embroidery. At the right is the
finished embroidery worked
by a student of the Royal School
of Needlework in London.

or use dressmaker's carbon paper which is available at notions departments. It comes in dark colors for light-colored fabric and light colors for dark fabrics. Note that it is quite difficult to get a good transfer on black fabric. White carbon paper, available in art supply stores, will often do the job.

Prick and Pounce Method

This method is included since it was one of the historic ways of transferring a design. It may be practical if you want to use the same design over and over. You will need firm tracing paper for the original tracing.

Insert the eye of a short needle in the eraser on the end of a pencil. Place your tracing on a soft surface such as newspapers or felt. Prick little holes along the lines of your design, making each prick quite close to the previous one and spacing them evenly. Prick the entire design.

Now tape the background fabric right side up to your work table and tape the pricking right side up on it. For light-colored fabrics you will need powdered charcoal (from a drugstore); for dark-colored fabrics, powdered chalk (used in skirt markers, available at a dressmaker's supply store). Cover your forefinger with a scrap of velvet or old terry towel; pick up some charcoal (or chalk) and rub through the pricking. Go over the entire design and then lift it off carefully. Although in the old method the design was finally painted in with a brush and watercolor paint, you will find it easier to draw it in with a pencil or a ball-point pen with waterproof ink.

Transfer Pattern Method

If you are not using an original design, the simplest way of obtaining a design is to use a transfer pattern which can be purchased in most department, hobby or variety stores. Transfer patterns can be used on smooth fabrics such as cotton or linen. Do not attempt to use them on velvets or highly textured fabrics.

Place the background fabric face up on your ironing board. (If the design is too large for your ironing board, use a large flat surface padded with a bath towel.) Fasten fabric with masking tape. Cut out

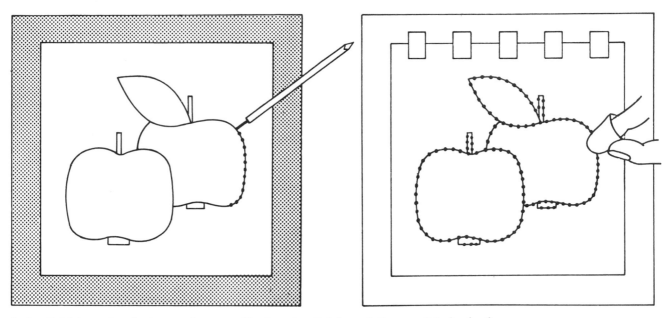

Left: Pricking the design with a needle for the Prick and Pounce Method of transferring a design. *Right:* Working the charcoal (or chalk) through the pricked design.

just those parts of the transfer you want to use. Blow away any loose flecks of the ink. Place the shiny (ink) side of the transfer in position facing down on your fabric; then tape. Make a test with a scrap of fabric and an extra piece of the transfer to check on the proper heat for your iron. "Low" or "Synthetic" settings are usually adequate. Do not glide the iron over the surface but use a stamping motion. Check your test piece to see if the transfer has taken. Then repeat the process on your background fabric. Peek under a corner of the transfer to see if it has taken. If not, repeat. Then run the warm iron over the surface of the pattern and quickly lift it off.

Hot Iron Pencil Method

A convenient way of transferring a design is to make your own transfer pattern with a copying (hectograph) pencil or "hot iron" pencil, carried by some needlework supply shops. First, make an exact tracing of your design. On the wrong side of the tracing, go over the entire design with the pencil. Keep pencil sharp so lines remain very fine. If you make a mistake, erase the line carefully since every line will transfer.

Now transfer your pattern to the background fabric (see Transfer Pattern Method, page 22) using an iron set at "Low" to "Medium."

23

Basting Method

Occasionally it is necessary to transfer a design to a fabric such as velvet or terry cloth which will not take a design by any of the above methods. The basting method is used in such cases. It can be done in two ways:

1. Transfer the design (by any method) to organdy or some other sheer fabric. Baste this in place on the right side of your napped background fabric and embroider right over the two fabrics. When the work is finished, cut off the excess organdy and carefully pull out the remaining organdy threads with tweezers.

2. An alternate method is to reverse the design and then transfer it to the organdy. Baste the organdy to the *wrong* side of your background fabric. With fine running stitches and sewing thread, go over all lines of the design so they appear on the *right* side of the background fabric. You can then use these lines as a basis for your embroidery. When the work is finished, clip away the excess organdy on the back of the work. This is the best way to work on a sweater or on any knit fabric.

Left: Embroidering directly over the design transferred to organdy which has been basted to right side of background fabric. *Right:* Using running stitches to transfer a design which has been applied to wrong side of background fabric.

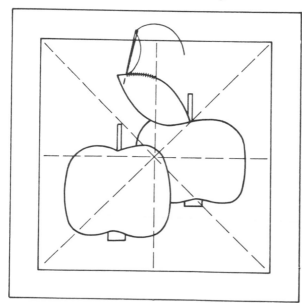
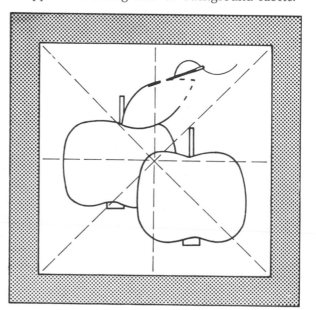

HOW TO ENLARGE AND REDUCE DESIGNS

To Make a Design Larger

Carry out the following method step by step and you'll soon have a pattern ready to use:

1. Use a large sheet of wrapping paper or the inexpensive art paper called newsprint. You'll also need a ruler and a sharp pencil.

2. Although you can work with any of the scale diagrams in this book, it is wise to practice with the little sample diagram given here first. Find out the exact scale and draw the number of squares indicated to the size of the scale. For example, in the diagram that follows the scale reads "Each small square = 1" square." In other words, on your paper draw 1" x 1" squares in the same number as the small diagram (or use 1" graph paper if available). You will notice that there are 4 squares across and 4 down in the small diagram.

3. Copy all lines from each square on the small diagram to its corresponding square on the graph you have drawn.

4. When you have completed all the squares, smooth out the lines, check your work for accuracy and you are ready to transfer the pattern to your fabric.

5. If you ever want to make an original or adapted design larger, do it in similar fashion. Draw a graph right on your own design. On another sheet of paper, draw an outline the exact size you want your new finished pattern to be. Then draw within this outline as many squares as you drew on your own design. Copy your design to your new graph as described in Step 3.

To Make a Design Smaller

Follow the above method but draw the graph squares smaller than those on your design.

An even simpler way of getting a perfect enlargement (or smaller version) of your design is to take it to a shop that makes copies and have it photostated. Indicate the size that you want your finished pattern to be. The shop will do the rest. The extra cost of a dollar or two is often worth the time you save. Copy the design on tracing paper before transferring it to the fabric.

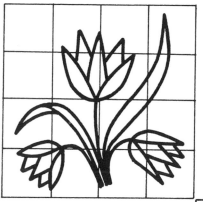

ENLARGING A DIAGRAM.
On small diagram each square
represents 1″ square; on large diagram
each square *is* 1″ square.

4. Success Tips for the Beginner

Be sure to thread your needle with the yarn going in the right direction. Yes, yarn has a right direction. Draw a strand through your fingers to determine in which direction it runs smoothly and in which direction you can feel the fibers. The yarn should go through the fabric so that the fibers are smooth—not roughed up. Thread your needle accordingly. Also, never thread your needle with one long strand and use it double. One half would be going in the wrong direction. If you want two strands of yarn, cut two pieces and have them both go in the same direction when threading your needle. Also remember to keep your strands fairly short (not over 18"), since long strands of yarn become frayed.

To thread a needle, fold the end of yarn over the needle, clasp the yarn tightly near the fold, then slip the yarn off the needle and insert the fold through the eye. (See diagram on page 28.)

When beginning a new piece of work, it is acceptable to make a knot in your yarn. However, many experts pride themselves on never making knots which will show on the back of their work. Instead, make a loose temporary knot and insert needle into right side of fabric a couple of inches from where you want to begin, leaving the loose knot on the *right* side of your work; bring needle up at the starting place and begin to embroider. End off the yarn by running it back under a few stitches on the *wrong* side of the work. Now

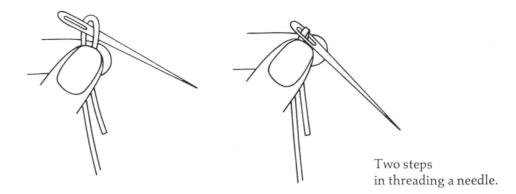

Two steps
in threading a needle.

undo the original knot and pull yarn to back of fabric; thread it into a needle and work under the first few stitches. Clip off ends. When beginning new yarns near a completed area, always run the new yarn under a few stitches.

Never carry your yarn for too great a distance when going from one area of the design to another. It is better to finish off and begin again.

When leaving your work, insert the attached needle and yarn into the background fabric so that they don't dangle. Just be sure that you keep it outside the area that is to be embroidered to avoid leaving needle holes in the fabric.

If you are working on a large project, much of which extends beyond your hoop, roll up and pin the excess to keep it clean and prevent wear.

When you are embroidering a garment that you are making yourself, first cut out the various pieces. Then embroider those pieces you want decorated with stitchery—sleeves or a neckline, for example—before you assemble the garment. Be sure to take into consideration seam allowances, darts, hems, etc. when planning your embroidery. For the border of a skirt it would be wise first to stitch the skirt seams, press them open and work the design right over them.

If you are decorating a ready-made garment, you may be able to remove the area to be worked, such as a pocket or belt. When this is not possible, slip a piece of cardboard under the area so that your stitches will not pierce the rest of the garment.

On any garment, be sure not to stretch or distort the area on your hoop or frame. It may be advisable in some cases not to use a hoop or frame at all.

28

5. A Glossary of Embroidery Stitches

Learning new embroidery stitches is a bit like learning geography: it opens up vistas of a wide, wide world. Geography makes travel more exciting, the daily newspaper more meaningful, even conversation takes on new overtones. The same is true of stitchery. New possibilities are open to you with every new stitch you learn.

If you are already a needleworker, learning crewel embroidery will help you enjoy your other crafts that much more. You will be able to add a lovely embroidered motif to your knitting or crocheting. If you do needlepoint, you will be able to embellish the finished work with crewel stitches that bring out the details. And if you are looking forward to learning other forms of needlework, your knowledge of crewel will stand you in good stead. Many of these same stitches are used in needlepoint, rug making, even lace making.

But don't get carried away by trying to learn a great many stitches at one time. It can be frustrating and confusing. Above all, don't read directions as literature. Directions should be worked step-by-step. Read a little and do what it tells you before reading on.

BEFORE YOU START

On your fabric, mark the lines or simple shapes on which to practice a specific stitch. Put fabric in a hoop and work the stitch following the directions.

The Needle Arts Bulletin of the Embroiderers' Guild of America offers this helpful suggestion for left-handed embroiderers: Trace the diagram on tracing paper, using a ball-point pen with black ink. Flip over the tracing and mark any letters that appear on the diagram in proper position. Keep the tracing of the diagram where you can refer to it easily.

SPECIAL NOTE: It appears in the stitch diagrams as if the needle goes in and out of the fabric in one step. Actually the needle should be inserted in a stabbing motion and pulled out in a separate operation. If you are a beginner and are using a hand-held hoop, it will be necessary for you to shift your right hand from the top to the underside of your work for each stitch. (If you are left-handed, you will hold the hoop with your right hand and stitch with your left.) As you become more experienced, or if you use a frame or a lap or floor hoop, insert the needle with the right hand and draw it through on the underside of the work with the left hand. On the next part of the stitch, push the needle upward with the left hand and draw it out with the right. Although this may seem a little awkward at first it makes for rhythmic work and an even stitch.

Learn a few basic stitches such as Running, Outline and Chain, French Knots and Satin Stitch. Then enjoy your newfound skill by making one of the simpler projects. You can add to your repertoire as you go along.

Certain stitches are rather complicated to remember. Almost everyone has to refer to written directions or a sampler for help when stitches haven't been worked for a while. In fact, it may be helpful to have a scrap of fabric in your work bag on which to practice and perfect a stitch before you begin a project.

All of the following stitches are numbered. These numbers are identical to the numbers on the working diagrams for each project throughout the book and furnish a ready reference.

After each stitch name, one or more small dots appear. These dots indicate the degree of difficulty of the stitch. They range from •, the easiest, to • • • • •, the most difficult. Remember, however, that some stitches, although easy to learn, take practice to do well.

Stitches are also listed under specific uses (pages 73 through 75).

(1) ARROWHEAD STITCH • •

A single row of these stitches is used for a medium-width line. A number of rows is used for a rather open filling. Work it from left to right. Bring needle up at A, insert it at B and up again at C. Insert at D just to the right of B. Make next stitch starting at E just to the right of C.

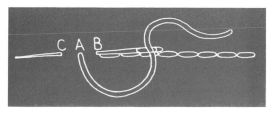

(2) BACKSTITCH •

This is one of the most useful stitches to know. It is used for line work of all kinds. Work it from right to left. Bring needle up near the beginning of the line to be covered at A, then insert it back at the beginning of the line at B. Bring needle out the same distance ahead along line at C and draw it through. Keep stitches evenly spaced and touching.

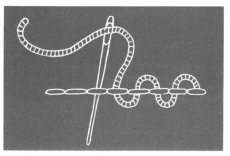

(2a) BACKSTITCH, SINGLE-THREADED •

This is used for more decorative lines or borders than plain Backstitch. Make a row of Backstitch then thread another color or kind of yarn under the Backstitches, keeping the needle and the yarn on top of the fabric. You may find it easier to use a blunt needle, or to insert the eye rather than the point of the needle under the stitch so it will not split the yarn. Threading that is tight will give a different effect from threading that is loose.

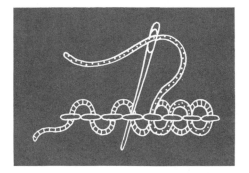
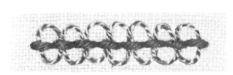

(2b) BACKSTITCH, DOUBLE-THREADED • •

This is even more decorative than Single-Threaded Backstitch. When you have completed a row of Backstitch and a row of single threading, work second row of threading, again keeping the needle and the yarn on top of the fabric so that loops are formed on the opposite side of those formed before. Threading may be done in the same color as the Backstitch or in a contrasting color.

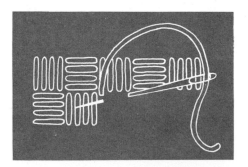
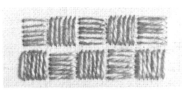

(3) BASKET FILLING STITCH • •

This makes a rather solid filling in fairly large areas. Make a block of desired number of vertical Satin Stitches. Now make a block of horizontal Satin Stitches of the same number. Repeat until area is completely filled. Satin Stitches may be worked close together or worked slightly apart as shown.

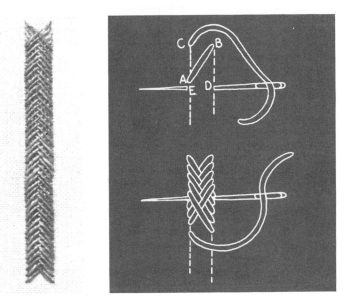

(4) BASKET STITCH • • •

Use this stitch for medium-width and wide lines. Draw two lines and work between them from the top down. Make an elongated Cross-Stitch AB and CD as in first diagram. Bring needle out at E (touching A). Make an overlapping Cross-Stitch as in second diagram. Continue.

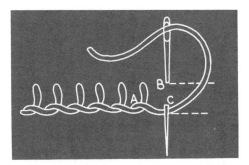

(5) BLANKET STITCH • •

Although this is regularly used to cover an edge, in crewel work it is used for outlining or for flowers when it is worked in a circle. Work it from left to right. Bring needle up on lower line at A. Hold yarn down with left thumb. Insert needle to the right above at B. Bring it out directly below on the lower line at C, pulling needle through over the loop of yarn. Repeat evenly across row. If this stitch seems a bit awkward to handle at first, try it without a hoop.

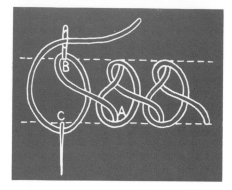

(6) BRAID STITCH • • • • •

This is used for borders. It is most effective when worked with heavy yarn. Draw two lines and work between them from right to left. Bring needle up on lower line at A. Make a yarn loop as in diagram; holding it down with left thumb, insert needle through loop at B and in fabric on top line. Tighten loop but do not pull so tight that the braid effect is lost. Bring needle out directly below on lower line at C. If this stitch seems a bit awkward to handle at first, try it without a hoop. Since this is a loose stitch, use it only on pieces that will not get hard usage or require washing.

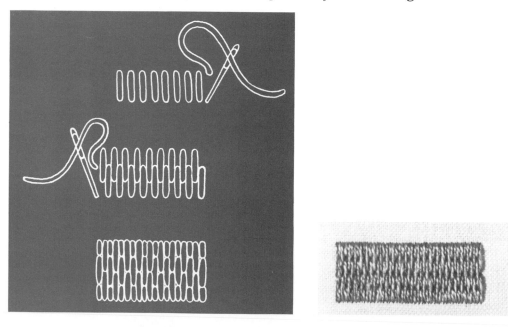

(7) BRICK STITCH • •

This stitch makes a solid filling. Work a Satin Stitch. Leaving the width of a stitch between, work next Satin Stitch. Repeat across area. Make a second row of stitches of the same size interlocking them with stitches of the first row as in the second step. Make number of rows necessary to fill area, then work top and bottom rows of stitches only half as tall, as shown, to fill in brick-like effect.

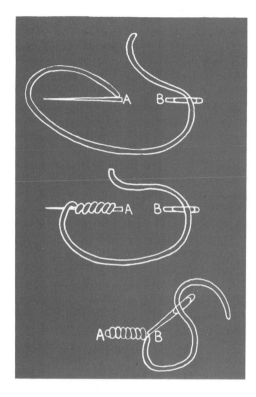

(8) BULLION STITCH • • • • •

Also known as Bullion Knots, these are used for heavy, encrusted effects particularly when worked in gold or silver. They may be used individually or worked in an overlapping circle to form a little flower. Bring yarn up at A, then insert needle in fabric at B, as far back as the distance of stitch desired but don't pull needle through. Now bring needle out where yarn first emerged at A, but *still* do not pull needle through fabric. Twist the yarn around the needle as many times as needed to fill the space of the stitch just taken. Hold left thumb on curled yarn and pull needle through. Pull needle and yarn to the right to tighten stitch. Then insert needle through fabric at B as in third diagram.

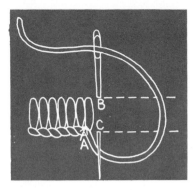

(9) BUTTONHOLE STITCH • •

A variation of the Blanket Stitch, this serves many of the same purposes. It is worked in the same fashion but the stitches are made closer together. Work it from left to right. Bring needle up on lower line at A. Hold yarn down with left thumb. Insert needle to the right above at B. Bring it out directly below on the lower line at C, pulling needle through over the loop of yarn. Repeat evenly across row. If stitch seems awkward to handle at first, try it without a hoop.

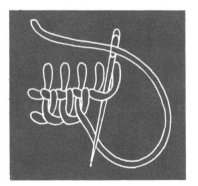

(10) BUTTONHOLE STITCH, DETACHED • • • •

Ordinary Buttonhole Stitch is called "attached" since it is worked into the fabric. For "detached" Buttonhole, work a row of ordinary Buttonhole Stitches. For the second row, bring needle up below beginning of preceding row, work Buttonhole Stitch but do not go into the fabric; rather, work each stitch into the little twist at the bottom of a stitch on the preceding row above. At end of each row, insert needle into fabric to anchor stitching and start next row at left. This can be worked for any number of rows. The stitches can be worked close together or spaced apart for a lacy effect. Another method of working Detached Buttonhole Stitch is to work the first row from left to right, the second row from right to left, etc.

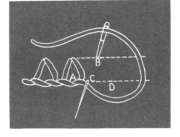

(11) BUTTONHOLE STITCH, CLOSED • • •

This is used for decorative borders. Work stitches in pairs so that the needle enters the fabric in the same place for each two stitches as follows: Work from left to right. Bring needle up on lower line at A. Hold yarn down with left thumb. Insert needle to the right above at B. Bring out at C, pulling needle over loop. Tighten stitch. Again hold yarn down with left thumb. Insert needle at B again but bring out at D, pulling needle over loop. To practice stitch, you may want to try it without a hoop.

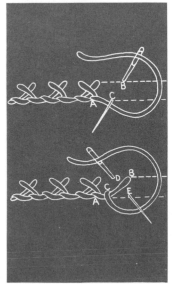

(12) BUTTONHOLE STITCH, CROSSED • • •

This is an even more decorative form of Buttonhole Stitch. Work from left to right. Bring needle up at A. Hold yarn down with left thumb. Insert needle at right above at B. Bring out at C, pulling needle over loop. Tighten stitch. Insert needle above at D and bring out at E. It may be easier to learn this stitch by working without hoop.

(13) CHAIN STITCH • •

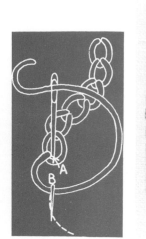

This is one of the most useful crewel stitches and is used for outlines. It also makes an excellent filling when worked in rows that just touch. When used for filling, all rows should be worked in the same direction. This stitch can be worked in heavy or lightweight yarn. The more intricate variations of the Chain Stitch that follow are often more effective when done in a lighter weight yarn. Work Chain Stitch from the top down. Bring needle to right side of fabric at A. Form a loop and hold it with left thumb. Insert needle where thread emerges back at A and bring it out a short distance below at B. Draw out over loop. At·end of a row, anchor last loop with a little stitch. When working Chain Stitch in a circle, interlock last stitch in first stitch to form a continuous chain. You may find it easier to learn this stitch by working without a hoop.

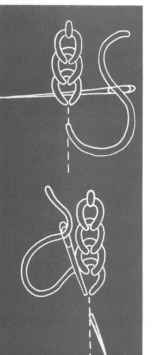

(14) CHAIN STITCH, BROAD • •

This variation of Chain Stitch is used for lines when a more solid effect is desired. Work it from top down. Make a small vertical stitch. Then bring needle out below. Run the needle under the vertical stitch without going into fabric and insert needle in same place it emerged, forming an upside-down loop. Bring needle out below. Continue, always running the needle under the last Chain Stitch made.

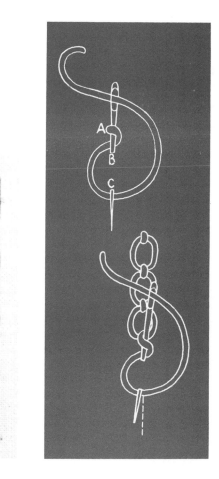

(15) CHAIN STITCH, CABLE • • •

This is used for the same purposes as the Chain Stitch, although it may be worked in slightly separated rows which can be laced together for a filling stitch. Bring needle up at top of line at A. Holding needle as shown, twist it around the yarn as for a French Knot. Pull yarn tight, insert needle into fabric at B. Form another Chain Stitch loop and draw needle out over loop at C. This stitch can also be worked in a zigzag (see Chain Stitch, Zigzag page 42).

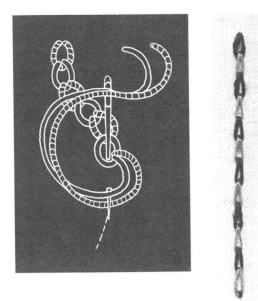

(16) CHAIN STITCH, CHECKERED • • • •

This is a stitch with which you can astound your friends since one color disappears with each stitch as if by magic. It is sometimes called a Magic Chain. Thread a needle with two colors of yarn. Work as for Chain Stitch, but when making the loops, pass one color under the needle and let the other color be on top of needle. Pull through both threads. Work next stitch, reversing the colors. If this stitch is a bit awkward to handle at first, try it without a hoop.

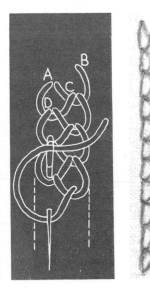

(17) CHAIN STITCH, DOUBLE • • • •

This makes a medium-width border. Work it from top down. Bring needle up at A; insert at B, forming an open loop. Bring needle out at C; insert at A, forming another loop. Bring needle out at D; then insert at C. Continue, alternating stitches from side to side. Be careful to keep loops of uniform size.

(18) CHAIN STITCH, HEAVY • •

This is used when a heavier effect than that produced by ordinary Chain Stitch is desired. Make a small vertical stitch at top of line. Bring needle out below this stitch. Thread yarn under this stitch without going into fabric. Insert needle in fabric where it last emerged. Bring it out below this point and again thread it under the vertical stitch. Insert needle in fabric where it last emerged. From this point on work each chain loop back under the two previous loops.

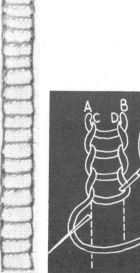

(19) CHAIN STITCH, OPEN • •

This is also called a Broad Chain, a Ladder Chain or a Roman Chain. Use it for medium or wide borders. It may even be made in a graduated width. Work it from the top down on two parallel lines. Bring needle out at A. Holding yarn with left thumb, insert needle at B, then bring it out just below A at C. Pull yarn through over loop. Leave loop slightly loose so that next stitch at D can be worked into it. Insert needle as in diagram and continue stitches from one side to the other. Secure last loop with a small stitch at each side.

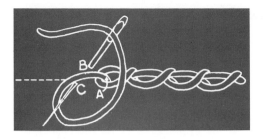

(20) CHAIN STITCH, TWISTED • •

This is a more decorative form of Chain Stitch. Work it from right to left. Work as for ordinary Chain Stitch, but instead of inserting needle into place from which it emerged, cross over the loop and work a slanting stitch (B-C) as in diagram. This stitch should be made with small loops to give the proper effect.

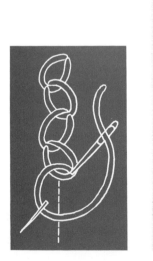

(21) CHAIN STITCH, ZIGZAG • •

This is a common variation of Chain Stitch. Work it from the top down. Work as for Chain Stitch but make each loop so that it is on the diagonal from the last loop. NOTE: Actually pierce the end of the preceding loop with the needle (rather than going inside the loop) so that each loop will be held in place.

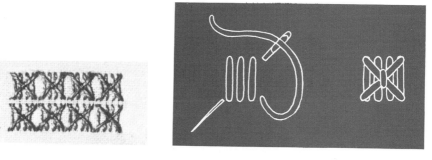

(22) CHESSBOARD FILLING STITCH • •

This forms a close or scattered filling, often used in large areas. Work Satin Stitches, spaced as shown or close together. Work a Cross-Stitch over the Satin Stitches. This may be tied down with a small stitch in the center as in diagram. These units may be alternated with open spaces of the same size to form a chessboard effect or they may be used more widely spaced.

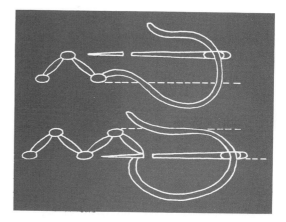

(23) CHEVRON STITCH • • •

This is useful for wide lines and can be used for a filling when rows of Chevron Stitch are grouped together. Work it from left to right between two parallel lines. Bring needle up on lower line and insert a short distance to the right. Bring needle out in center of stitch just formed, being careful not to split the yarn. Next, insert needle on the upper line a little to the right and bring needle up a short distance to the left (top part of diagram). Insert needle to the right on same line and bring it up in the center of the stitch just formed. Work alternately on lower and upper lines.

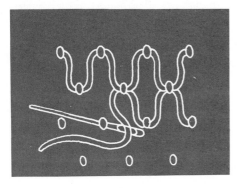

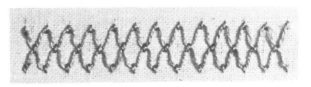

(24) CLOUD FILLING STITCH • • •

This makes a lacy filling for large areas. With double yarn, work small stitches over entire area staggering them from row to row. Space very evenly. Using a blunt needle, lace through these stitches with a single yarn working between the top two rows first. Next work the third row up into the second row. Loops meet as in diagram. This stitch is most effective when worked in two contrasting colors or in different weights of yarn.

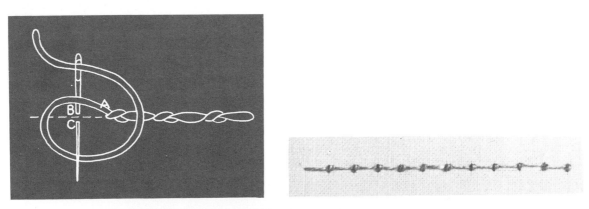

(25) CORAL STITCH • • •

This is a basic line stitch. Double yarn is preferable. Work it from right to left. Bring yarn up at right of line at A. Holding down yarn with left thumb, make a little vertical stitch B-C across the line. Be sure needle is under, then over, yarn as in diagram. Keep knots evenly spaced and fairly close together. This is a stitch that you may want to practice without a hoop until you learn how to do it.

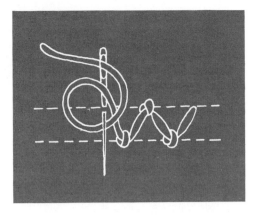

(26) CORAL STITCH, ZIGZAG • • •

This is used for borders rather than lines. Working as for Coral Stitch, make a stitch on top line, then on lower line.

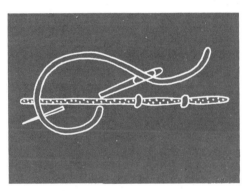

(27) COUCHING STITCH • •

This is a basic line stitch. Thread one or more strands in a large-eyed needle. Fasten at underside at right end of line to be worked. Draw through and lay strands along line. Hold strands with left hand. With a single strand in the needle, work small stitches, evenly spaced, to hold down the laid strands. At end of row draw all strands to back of work and fasten off. Couching can be converted to a close filling stitch by working the couched line back and forth in straight close rows. It can also be used as an open filling by zig-zagging the couching line all over the area in a free manner (known as Random Couching).

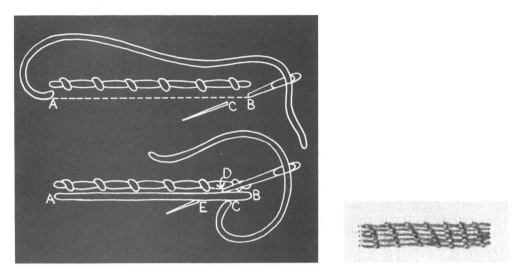

(28) COUCHING STITCH, BOKHARA • •

This is a solid filling stitch. Although it is worked like regular Couching, the same strand is used for both the laid-down stitch and the tying-down stitches. Bring yarn up on left at A and carry across the space; insert needle on right at B. Work evenly spaced small stitches (C to D, etc.) across the laid strand. Repeat by carrying across second strand close to the first. Make all tying-down stitches rather tight and close and neatly related to those on preceding row.

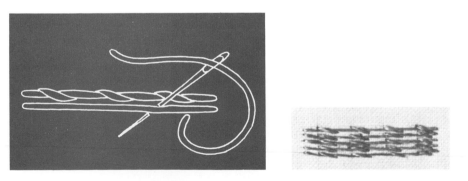

(29) COUCHING STITCH, RUMANIAN • •

This is also a solid filling stitch. Work as for Bokhara Couching but make the tying-down stitches longer and more slanting.

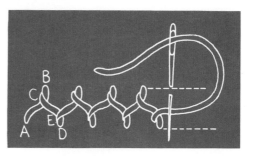

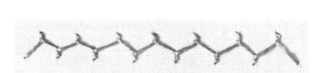

(30) CRETAN STITCH, OPEN • • •

This stitch is used for borders or for open fillings. It may be worked all one width, as shown, or in a graduated width (from narrow to wide then back to narrow as in an openwork leaf). Work it from left to right. Start by bringing needle up on lower line at A. Work a small vertical stitch a little to the right on top line B to C, needle pointing down. Be sure yarn is looped under needle. Then work a small vertical stitch D to E on lower line, needle pointing up. Be sure yarn is looped under needle. This is a stitch that you may want to practice without a hoop until you learn how to do it.

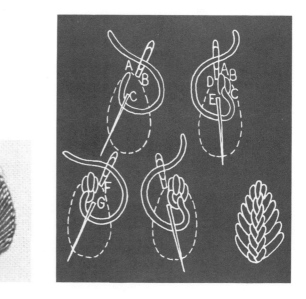

(31) CRETAN STITCH, LEAF • • • •

Bring yarn out at A, then make a small stitch from B to C (near center of leaf), coming out over the loop. Go down at D and up at E (near center of leaf) and bring needle out over the loop. Continue from side to side, repeating the last two steps. Keep the stitches close together along edges to maintain the slant of the yarn. To learn this stitch more easily, try working without a hoop.

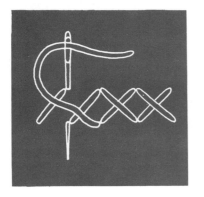

(32) CROSS-STITCH • •

A multipurpose stitch, this is used for borders and light or solid fillings. This stitch is worked in two steps. Work first step from left to right, the last step from right to left. Bring yarn out at lower left corner of a stitch and make a diagonal stitch, inserting needle in upper right corner. Repeat across, making each stitch the same size. On second step, work back over stitches as in diagram. Note that all stitches cross in the same direction.

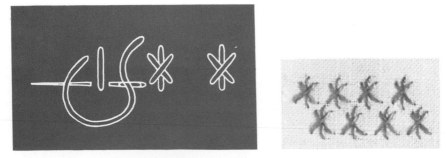

(33) ERMINE FILLING STITCH • •

This makes a light filling. Work a long center stitch, then top with a long-armed Cross-Stitch.

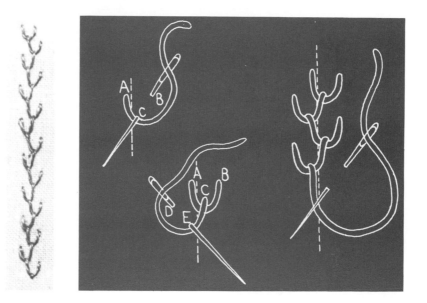

(34) FEATHER STITCH • • •

A multipurpose stitch, this is used for borders, lacy leaves and light filling. Work it from the top down. Bring needle up slightly to left of guideline at A. Holding yarn down with left thumb, work a slanting stitch to the right of the guideline at B and slightly below the beginning point (with needle pointing left and coming out near guideline at C). Draw needle out over yarn. Now, making a loop to the left and working on left side of guideline, make a similar stitch D-E with needle pointing to the right, coming out near guideline again. Draw needle out over yarn. To learn this stitch more easily, you may want to practice it without a hoop.

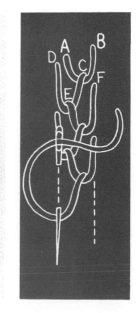

(35) FEATHER STITCH, CLOSED • • •

This is used for borders. Work it from the top down on two parallel lines. Bring needle up at A. Insert at B and bring needle out at C, keeping yarn under needle. Always hold needle perpendicularly. Insert needle just below A at D and make a similar stitch only on the left side. Alternate from side to side, making stitches close together. When you are learning this stitch, you may find it easier to practice without a hoop.

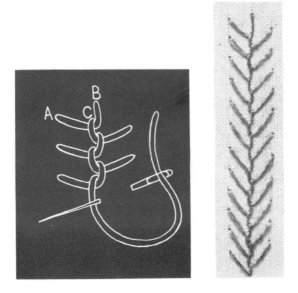

(36) FEATHER STITCH, LONG-ARMED • • •
This forms a wide border. Work it from the top down. Bring needle up at A. Insert needle at B, bring up at C, drawing needle over yarn. Make a similar stitch to right. Alternate stitches from left to right. If this stitch seems a bit awkward at first, try practicing it without a hoop.

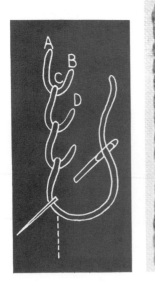

(37) FEATHER STITCH, SINGLE • • •
This is used for lines. Work it from the top down. Bring needle up at A. Holding yarn with left thumb, make a slanting stitch B to C on the right side of guideline. Draw needle through over yarn. Stitches may be made on left or right but should be on same side throughout. To learn this stitch more easily, you may want to practice it without a hoop.

(38) FERN STITCH • • •

Use this stitch for lacy leaves or as veining for leaves. Make three straight stitches of equal length, all radiating from the same point. Make next group of three stitches directly below. Note how center stitch of each group of three stitches forms a connected line.

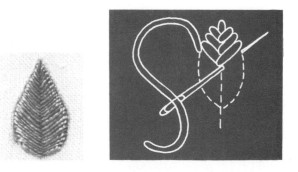

(39) FISHBONE STITCH • • •

This stitch fills in small shapes solidly. Make a small stitch at top of center line. Bring needle up on left edge of shape. Insert needle a little below first stitch, crossing center line. Bring out on right edge of shape. Work a similar stitch crossing to the left of center line, then bring needle out on left edge. Alternate stitches from left to right.

(40) FISHBONE STITCH, RAISED • • • •

In appearance this stitch is just like the Fishbone Stitch but it is thicker and looks padded. Work one long vertical stitch (A-B), then make a long-armed Cross-Stitch (C-D and E-F) on top of it. Bring thread up on left edge of shape at G in second diagram. Insert needle above at H then bring it out directly opposite at I. Insert needle on right edge below lowest stitch and bring out directly opposite (see third diagram). Repeat these two parts of stitch until shape is filled.

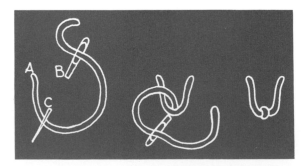

(41) FLY STITCH • •

This is a versatile stitch which can be used in rows for borders or for filling. Bring needle up at left corner of stitch at A and insert at upper right at B. Then bring needle out at center below, C, drawing it through over the loop just formed. Tie down loop with a small stitch.

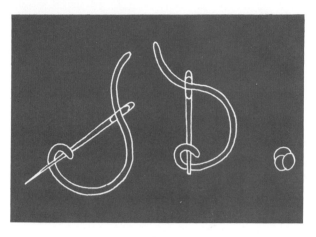

(42) FRENCH KNOT • •

This stitch may be used singly for a dot, in rows for a line, scattered for a filling or grouped, as for a flower center. Bring needle up. Pass the needle around the yarn *once*, then insert it back close to where yarn emerged but not in exact hole. Keep even tension on yarn wound on needle. Pull yarn to wrong side, holding knot in place. For large knots use two or three strands of yarn or a larger needle. Never pass the needle around the yarn more than once.

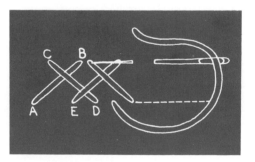

(43) HERRINGBONE STITCH • • •

This forms a border. Work it from left to right. Bring needle out at A, insert it at B. Bring needle out again at C, insert it at D and bring it out at E. Continue across row.

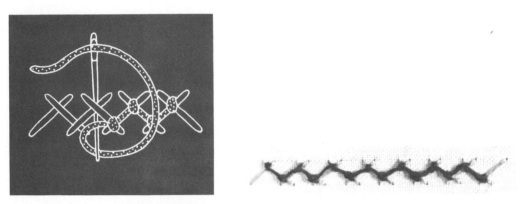

(44) HERRINGBONE STITCH, TIED • • •

This is just one of the many ways of decorating a row of Herring-bone Stitches. With a tapestry needle, work a row of Coral Stitches, making a knot at each point where Herringbone Stitches cross. Do not stick needle through fabric when making the knots.

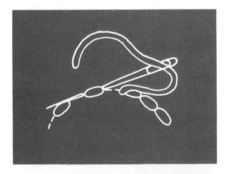

(45) HOLBEIN STITCH •

This is used for lines and outlines. Since it is similar in effect to the Backstitch, it can also be used as a foundation for threaded stitches. Work a row of Running Stitches along guideline, making each stitch and each space between of identical size. Now work Running Stitch back over the line, filling in all the spaces either with the same color or with a second color.

(46) HONEYCOMB FILLING STITCH • • • •

This is a decorative filling, often more effective when worked in heavier yarns. Using Laid Stitch, make long, evenly spaced horizontal stitches over the shape to be filled. Then work evenly spaced diagonal stitches over the horizontal ones. With a tapestry needle, weave in diagonal stitches in the other direction. Weave over and under as in diagram.

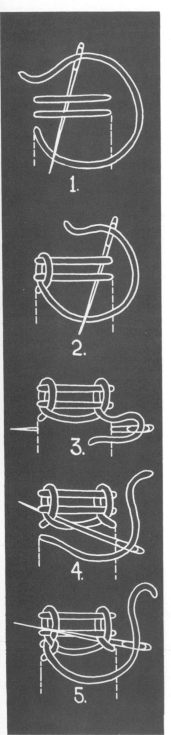

(47) *LADDER STITCH* • • • • •

This forms a border. Work it from the top down between two parallel lines. Make two horizontal stitches. Without going into fabric, pass needle under the two stitches making a loop stitch (diagram 1). Repeat on right side (diagram 2). Insert needle in right line, bring out on left line (diagram 3). Insert needle between second and third rungs of ladder, pass it under both strands of left loop and draw through (diagram 4). Repeat on right loop (diagram 5). Continue, following diagrams 3, 4 and 5. Keep stitches even.

(48) LAID STITCH • •

The appearance of this stitch is exactly like Satin Stitch but it uses much less yarn. Work a Satin Stitch across the shape to be filled but do not go back to starting edge. Make a little stitch as in diagram, leaving the width of a stitch between the two stitches. Work entire shape with these spaced stitches, then work back over the shape filling in the open spaces.

(49) LAID WORK, TIED • • • •

This is used for solid filling when a very decorative effect is desired. Fill in entire shape in Laid Stitch. Work diagonal stitches over the Laid Stitches. Make a second series of diagonal stitches in the opposite direction. Tie down the diagonal stitches where they cross with a little stitch.

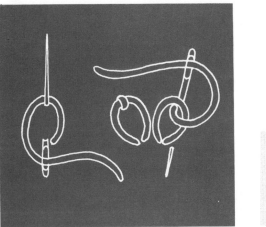

(50) LAZY-DAISY STITCH • •

This is also called Detached Chain Stitch. Worked in a circle, these stitches form a flower. Scattered, they make a light filling. Bring yarn up and hold with left thumb. Insert needle close to where yarn emerged. Then bring it out the desired length of stitch. Draw out over loop. Tie down with a small stitch over the loop.

(51) LAZY-DAISY STITCH, LONG-TAILED • •

Work as for Lazy-Daisy Stitch but make the loops smaller and the tying-down stitch longer.

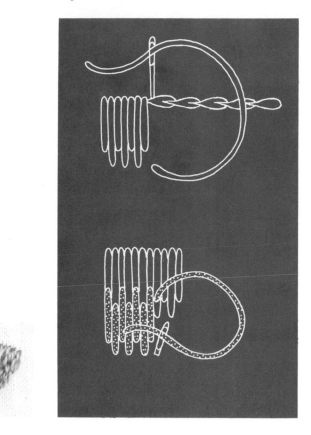

(52) LONG AND SHORT STITCH • • • •

This is used to fill a shape that is too large for Satin Stitch or where a very delicately shaded effect is desired. It separates the needlework experts from the tyros since it is difficult to do well although the technique is simple. First, pad the outline with a row of Split Stitches. Then work the top row with Satin Stitch, alternating a long and a short stitch. The next row is worked with the stitches coming up into the stitches of the previous row and may slightly overlap them. Continue rows as needed to fill the space using closely related shades of one color.

Keep stitches close. If necessary add a small wedge-shaped stitch to fill in the wide part when going around curves. It is also wise to pencil in on your fabric the direction of your stitches on curved shapes. Note that the stitches of the second row are all the same length but they are staggered. Actually only the first and last rows are long and short.

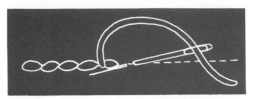 

(53) OUTLINE STITCH •

This is a basic crewel stitch. Work it from left to right. Bring needle up at end of guideline and insert it a little to the right. Bring needle out a little to the left and at a slight angle (not quite touching previous stitch). Always keep the yarn above the needle. This stitch can be worked as a solid filling when worked in close rows. Always work close rows in the same direction.

(54) OVERCAST STITCH • •

Use this stitch for outlines and fine but pronounced lines. Work a row of Running Stitches along guideline. Then work a row of tiny Satin Stitches across these stitches, picking up as little fabric as possible. Sometimes this is worked over a laid cord and is then known as Trailing.

(55) PEKINGESE STITCH • •

This stitch forms a decorative border or filling. Work a row of Backstitches. Working with a yarn of another color, interlace into the Backstitches as in diagram. Do not let lacing go through the fabric.

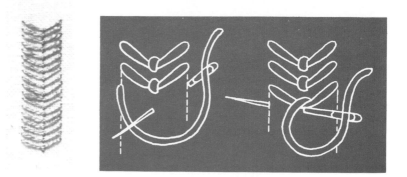

(56) ROMAN STITCH • •

This is an effective stitch for borders or filling. Work it from the top down between two lines. Bring needle up on left line and insert directly opposite on right line. Bring needle out in center and make a small stitch over the loop; then bring needle out on left line.

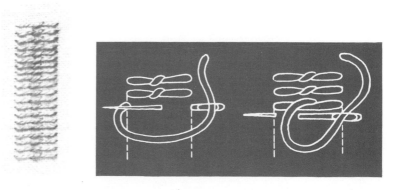

(57) RUMANIAN STITCH • •

This is used for borders or filling. Work it from the top down between two lines. Bring needle up on left line. Make a Satin Stitch across the space. Tie down with a small slanting stitch in the center. Work stitches very closely so no fabric shows.

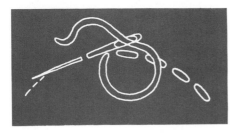

(58) RUNNING STITCH •

This forms a simple line or outline. Work stitch from right to left. Keep stitches all the same size and evenly spaced. Remember to work each stitch separately—not a few stitches at a time as in sewing. Work in close rows for a filling. For a threaded Running Stitch, work threading as for Backstitch, Single-Threaded, or Backstitch, Double-Threaded.

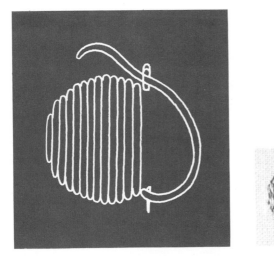

(59) SATIN STITCH • •

This is a solid filling stitch and should not be worked over too wide an area. Take a long stitch across the space. Return to starting edge and repeat. Work stitches in any direction but keep them parallel and close together. For a neat edge, the shape may be outlined first with Running, Back or Split Stitches, then the Satin Stitch worked over it. When working a shape such as a leaf, start at the center and work out to the point. Then return to the center and work out to the opposite point.

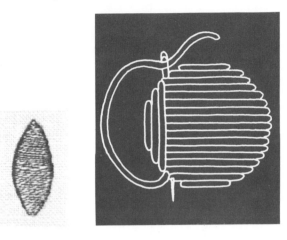

(60) SATIN STITCH, PADDED • • •

For a nice puffy effect, use padding stitches before doing the Satin Stitching. Use Satin Stitch as shown or Chain or Split Stitch. Always work the padding stitches in the opposite direction to that which you are going to work the final Satin Stitch. Photograph shows that Padded Satin Stitch can be worked in a variety of shapes.

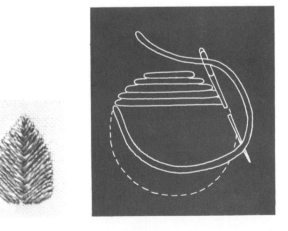

(61) SATIN STITCH, SURFACE • • •

Use this stitch when you want to save yarn. Do not return underneath the fabric to the starting edge for each stitch. Make a small stitch at the edge, then make a small stitch at the opposite edge. Laid Stitch is recommended for this purpose, however, when close stitches are desired. Note in photograph how an area is worked in sections to create a leaflike effect.

(62) SCROLL STITCH • • •

This forms a narrow border. It is most effective when worked with heavier yarn. Work it from left to right. Bring needle up at left end of guideline. Make a loop of yarn as in diagram. In the center of the loop make a tiny stitch slanting slightly to the left. Pull loop, then draw needle out over loop. Space stitches evenly. You may find it easier to practice this stitch without a hoop.

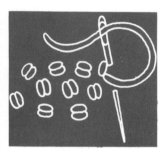

(63) SEED STITCH •

Also known as Seeding, this is used as a light filling and may be made scattered or quite dense. Make a tiny stitch, then make another stitch right next to it. Do not pull yarn too tight. Stitches should go in all directions.

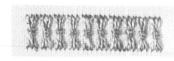

(64) SHEAF FILLING STITCH • •

This is a common filling stitch. Work three vertical Satin Stitches, then bring needle out at center as shown. Make two small stitches over the

Satin Stitches, without going into fabric, then insert needle where thread emerged. Sheaves may be lined up in horizontal rows or worked in staggered rows.

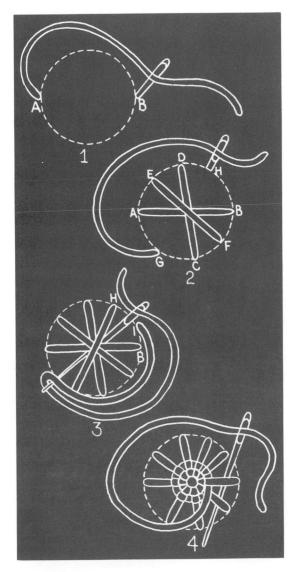

(65) SPIDER WEB, WHIPPED • • • • •

This is generally used sparingly as a particularly interesting detail. Using a tapestry needle bring yarn out at A, then insert at B (diagram 1). Then bring needle out at C and insert at D (line C-D is not quite vertical). Bring needle out at E and insert at F. Bring needle out at G and insert at H (note that H is closer to D than B in diagram 2). Bring needle out at I (halfway between H and B). Do not insert needle in fabric but run it under all strands at the center. Loop yarn over needle as in diagram 3. Pull needle through and straight up. This will knot the strands together in center.

Working clockwise, run needle under two strands at the center, then run needle under the last strand used and under one new strand (diagram 4). Repeat this step, going back over one strand and running needle under two strands until spokes are whipped the desired amount. Edge of Spider Web may be outlined with Stem Stitch, Holbein or Backstitch.

(66) SPIDER WEB, WOVEN • • • • •

This is used in the same way as the Whipped Spider Web. Following diagrams 1, 2 and 3 for the Whipped Spider Web, work until the spokes have been knotted together at the center (diagram 3). Continuing clockwise with the same working yarn, weave under one spoke, over one spoke until desired amount of web is filled. Don't go through the fabric.

(67) SPLIT STITCH •

This is used for lines, as padding for Satin Stitch and, when worked in close lines, as a filling. It resembles a fine Chain Stitch but is worked like Stem Stitch. Work it from left to right. Make a small stitch backward and pierce the yarn with the needle as shown.

(68) STAR FILLING STITCH • •

This forms an open filling. Make a Cross-Stitch with the arms on the vertical and horizontal as shown. Make a second Cross-Stitch in normal (X-shape) position over the first. Tie the first two together with a tiny Cross-Stitch worked over the intersection.

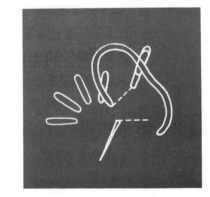

(69) STEM STITCH •

This is similar to Outline Stitch and worked in the same way except that the thread is held *below* the needle as shown.

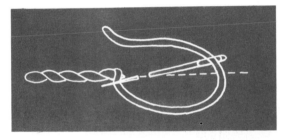

(70) STRAIGHT STITCH •

Use this stitch as an individual line in a design or as part of a group. The diagram is self-explanatory.

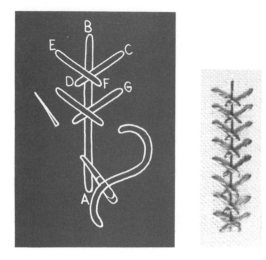

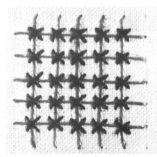

(71) THORN STITCH • •

This is used for leaves or veins in leaves. Make a long stitch from bottom A to top B across space to be worked. Now, working from the top down, make diagonal stitches *crossing over* the long stitch, following letters in sequence as in diagram.

(72) TRELLIS STITCH • • •

A filling stitch common in crewel embroidery, this is also known as Jacobean Couching. Make long horizontal stitches evenly spaced across shape. Make vertical stitches across the horizontal stitches. Then work a half Cross-Stitch or a whole Cross-Stitch to tie down the yarns at each intersection. There are many variations to this stitch. A large Cross-Stitch, a French Knot or a Lazy-Daisy Stitch can be worked in each open space.

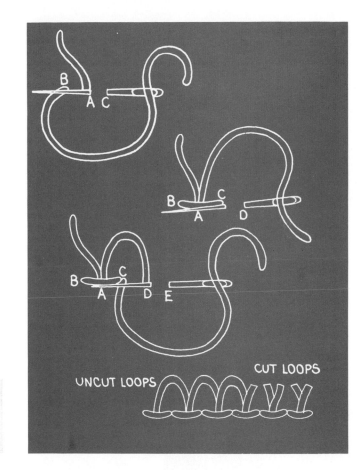

(73) TURKEY WORK • • • • •

Use this stitch as a solid filling when a velvety pile is desired. It is most effective when several strands of yarn, or a heavier yarn, is used. Work it in horizontal rows from left to right. Leaving 1" of yarn on top of work, insert needle at A, come up at B. With yarn *below* needle, insert it at C and come up in same hole as A. Draw stitch tight, holding end of thread so it does not pull through. With yarn *above* needle, insert it at D, come up in same hole as C. Leave a loop as in diagram. (The size of the loop depends on the height of the pile you want.) With yarn *below* needle, insert at E and come up back at D. Pull stitch tight. Continue, alternately making a loop and an anchoring stitch. Make enough rows (close together) to fill the area completely, then shear off the top of the stitches. Turkey Work can be left uncut, sheared flat or contoured to fit the design.

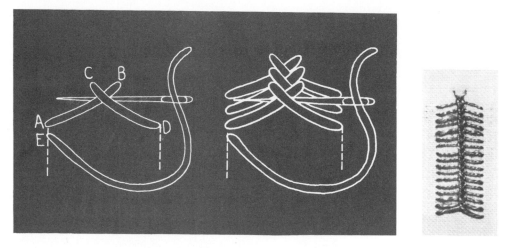

(74) VANDYKE STITCH • • • •

This makes a border. Work between two parallel lines. Bring needle up at A, insert at B and bring out at C. Now insert needle at D and bring out at E. Without piercing fabric, slide needle under the center crossed stitches; draw through. Insert needle in right edge below D and bring out on left edge below E. Slide needle under the last crossed stitch. Repeat steps described in last two sentences. Stitches may be worked close together or just slightly separated.

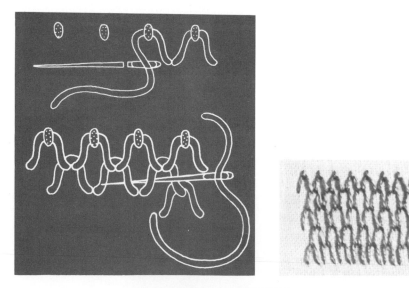

(75) WAVE STITCH • • •

This forms an open filling. Working from left to right, make a row of small vertical stitches. Bring needle up at right edge below these stitches. Slip needle under first stitch above, and without piercing fabric, draw through without pulling yarn too tightly. Make a small horizontal stitch below on a line with point where yarn last emerged. Now work under next stitch. In the third and all subsequent rows, slip the needle under the legs of the two stitches immediately above (as in diagram).

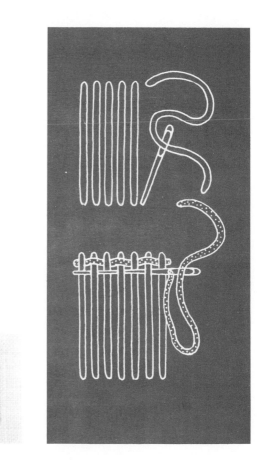

(76) WEAVING STITCH • • •

This is a basic filling stitch worked just like darning. Using Laid Stitch, make vertical stitches across area to be filled. With a tapestry needle and a contrasting color if desired, weave under and over the yarns, going down into the fabric only at the beginning and end of each row. It is sometimes easier to begin weaving at the center. Then work to the top, return to the center, and work to the bottom.

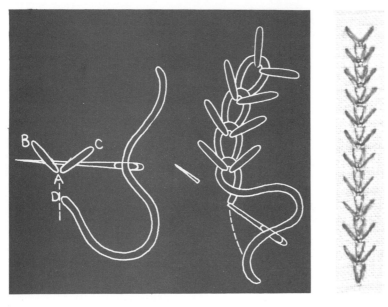

(77) WHEAT-EAR STITCH • • •

This is used for borders or stems. Work it from the top down. Bring needle up on guideline at A, insert at B and bring out at C. Now insert needle close to A again and bring out a distance below at D (as in first diagram). Without piercing fabric, slip needle under the first two stitches (see first diagram). Insert needle in spot where yarn last emerged and bring out to left (as in second diagram). Make two more straight stitches. Alternate loop stitch with two straight stitches.

Specific Uses for Embroidery Stitches

Note: Stitches are coded according to degree of difficulty. (See page 30)

Narrow Lines

Backstitch (.)

Backstitch, Single-Threaded (.)

Backstitch, Double-Threaded (..)

Bullion Stitch (worked in a line) (.....)

Chain Stitch (..)

Chain Stitch, Broad (..)

Chain Stitch, Cable (...)

Chain Stitch, Checkered (....)

Chain Stitch, Heavy (..)

Chain Stitch, Twisted (..)

Coral Stitch (...)

Couching Stitch (..)

Feather Stitch, Single (...)

French Knot (worked in a line) (..)

Holbein Stitch (.)

Outline Stitch (.)

Overcast Stitch (..)

Running Stitch (.)

Scroll Stitch (...)

Split Stitch (.)

Stem Stitch (.)

Straight Stitch (.)

Medium and Wide Lines and Borders

Arrowhead Stitch (..)

Basket Stitch (...)

Blanket Stitch (..)

Braid Stitch (.....)

Buttonhole Stitch (..)

Buttonhole Stitch, Closed (...)

Buttonhole Stitch, Crossed (...)

Chain Stitch, Double (....)

Chain Stitch, Open (..)

Chain Stitch, Zigzag (..)

Chevron Stitch (...)

Coral Stitch, Zigzag (...)

Cretan Stitch, Open (...)

Cross-Stitch (..)

Feather Stitch (...)

Feather Stitch, Closed (...)

Feather Stitch, Long-Armed (...)

Fern Stitch (...)

Fly Stitch (..)

Herringbone Stitch (...)

Herringbone Stitch, Tied (...)

Ladder Stitch (.....)

Medium and Wide Lines and Borders (continued)

Pekingese Stitch (. .)   Vandyke Stitch (. . . .)
Roman Stitch (. .)   Wheat-Ear Stitch (. . .)
Rumanian Stitch (. .)

Open Filling

Arrowhead Stitch (. .)   Honeycomb Filling Stitch (. . . .)
Bullion Stitch (. . . . .)   Lazy-Daisy Stitch (. .)
Buttonhole Stitch, Detached (. . . .) Lazy-Daisy Stitch, Long-Tailed (. .)
Chessboard Filling Stitch (. .)   Pekingese Stitch (. .)
Chevron Stitch (. . .)   Running Stitch (.)
Cloud Filling Stitch (. . .)   Seed Stitch (.)
Couching Stitch (. .)   Sheaf Filling Stitch (. .)
Cretan Stitch, Open (. . .)   Star Filling Stitch (. .)
Cross-Stitch (. .)   Straight Stitch (.)
Ermine Filling Stitch (. .)   Thorn Stitch (. .)
Feather Stitch (. . .)   Trellis Stitch (. . .)
Fly Stitch (. .)   Wave Stitch (. . .)
French Knot (. .)

Solid Filling

Basket Filling Stitch (. .)   Couching Stitch (. .)
Brick Stitch (. .)   Couching Stitch, Bokhara (. .)
Bullion Stitch (. . . . .)   Couching Stitch, Rumanian (. .)
Buttonhole Stitch, Detached (. . . .) Cretan Stitch, Leaf (. . . .)
Chain Stitch (. .)   Cross-Stitch (. .)
Chessboard Filling Stitch (. .)   Fishbone Stitch (. . .)

Solid Filling (continued)

Fishbone Stitch, Raised (. . . .)

Fly Stitch (. .)

French Knot (. .)

Laid Stitch (. .)

Laid Work, Tied (. . . .)

Long and Short Stitch (. . . .)

Outline Stitch (.)

Roman Stitch (. .)

Rumanian Stitch (. .)

Satin Stitch (. .)

Satin Stitch, Padded (. . .)

Satin Stitch, Surface (. . .)

Spider Web, Whipped (. . . . .)

Spider Web, Woven (. . . . .)

Split Stitch (.)

Stem Stitch (.)

Turkey Work (. . . . .)

Weaving Stitch (. . .)

Small Spots

Bullion Stitch (. . . . .)

French Knot (. .)

Lazy-Daisy Stitch (. .)

Seed Stitch (.)

Straight Stitch (.)

Note on the Projects That Follow

For all the projects that follow, except Accent Crewel (page 96), a diagram is given for the embroidery design. Whenever space allows, the diagram is actual size. When a diagram is not actual size, it is shown on a graph so that you can enlarge it (see page 25).

On most of the diagrams you will find letters and numbers. Each letter refers to the color that you should use on a particular area of your embroidery. The key to follow is shown right on the diagram. The numbers refer to the stitches to be used. You can check these in the Glossary of Embroidery Stitches which begins on page 29.

Letters or numbers (or both) have been omitted from some diagrams; in these cases, the details have been included in the directions for that particular project. Sometimes this was done because the stitches needed a few words of explanation or the number of symbols required would have made the diagram too crowded to follow easily. In any case, the method chosen was to make your embroidery as easy and enjoyable as possible.

The projects have been selected to give you an opportunity to use a wide variety of stitches and designs. You can follow the directions exactly and make the piece as it is photographed, or you can adapt the design or choose a part of it to use in some other way. You will find suggestions for other uses at the beginning of each project, but don't stop there. Creating your own uses for a design is one of the most satisfying ways to add to the many pleasures of crewel.

6. Projects for Beginners

Song of the Sea Sampler

It's so easy to think of a sampler as an 1817 embroidered verse with an alphabet and a few traditional symbols that we forget the original meaning of the word. A sampler is simply a record of stitches or small patterns and that is exactly what this framed picture is. It gives you a chance to work all the major line stitches for both practice and ready reference. Eleven basic crewel stitches are included in this project.

If you prefer to work a sampler without using this particular pattern, you will gain the same experience by just drawing straight lines or using a striped fabric on which to practice these line stitches. If you are working on stripes you might also add any number of the wide-line stitches found in the chart on pages 73 and 74 described in the Glossary of Embroidery Stitches (page 29).

Song of the Sea Sampler makes a fine learning project for beginners.

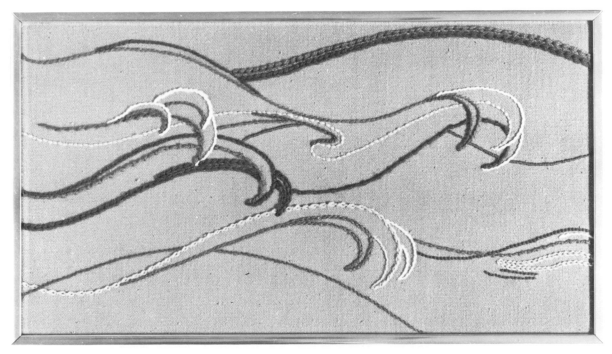

[Song of the Sea Sampler]

Size:
Finished sampler, 10″ x 18″

Materials:
½ yard homespun-type cotton
Small amounts (a few yards) of white yarn and about five
    different weights of yarn in shades of blue
10″ x 18″ piece of heavy cardboard
Picture frame with 9½″ x 17½″ opening
9½″ x 17½″ piece of ¼″-thick foam rubber
Masking tape
White glue

Pattern:
Enlarge diagram for pattern (each small square = 1″
square). Or draw your own waves. Transfer design to a
piece of fabric cut 16″ x 24″.

Working Method:
Place work in an embroidery hoop or frame. Use light
shades of blue at top of waves, darker shades at bottom of
waves, white on the crests of the waves. Use the following
line stitches: Outline (53), Stem (69), Holbein (45), Chain
(13), Split (67), Twisted Chain (20), Coral (25), Scroll (62),
Backstitch (2), Couching (27) and Overcast (54). (Numbers
refer to stitches listed in Glossary, page 29.) These can be
worked over any of the lines on your design and in any
order.

Finishing:
Block, then cut sampler to 12″ x 21″. Finish following directions for Framing a Picture (page 153).

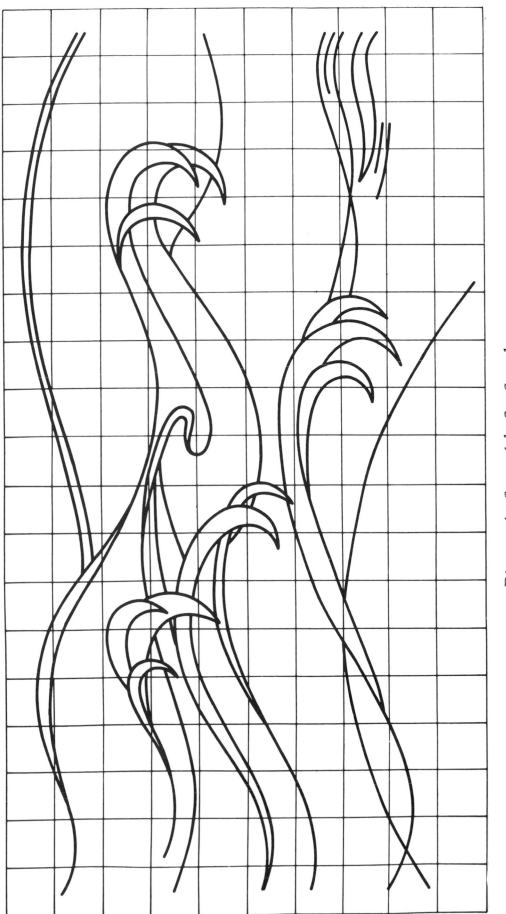

Diagram for Song of the Sea Sampler.

Twining Vine Bookmark

Here is a simple little design that gives you a chance to develop two basic stitches in such a pretty—and easy—way that you may decide to make a half dozen of these bookmarks as gifts or for your next bazaar.

This design could also be used to ornament an eyeglass case or as a border down each side of an envelope purse or tote bag. You can extend it, using a longer piece of linen to make a headband or a belt. Or enlarge it (and work it on a longer, wider piece of linen) for a bell pull or a guitar strap.

[Bookmark]

Size:
8" long, excluding tassel

Materials:
Scrap of natural color linen
Crewel wool, a few yards each of dark green, light green and magenta
Scrap of lightweight interfacing or muslin

Pattern:
Trace the diagram (shown actual size). Transfer to background fabric large enough to fit in your embroidery hoop.

Working Method:
Place work in hoop. Use one strand of wool throughout. First work stem in dark green Stem Stitch (69); then embroider leaves in light green Stem Stitch. Work line around edge in magenta Stem Stitch, little circles in magenta French Knots (42). (Numbers refer to stitches listed in Glossary, page 29.)

Finishing:
Cut out embroidered piece, leaving ¼" seam allowance all around. Cut out same-size backing piece of linen and same-

size interfacing piece. Baste interfacing piece to back of embroidered piece. Right sides together, stitch embroidered piece to backing piece, leaving a 2″ opening on one side. Trim seams, clip corners and turn bookmark right side out. Slip-stitch opening closed (see page 152). Press carefully.

For tassel, wrap magenta wool twenty times around a 2½″ piece of cardboard. Slip off and tie strands together at one end. Sew this end to point of bookmark. Wrap and tie tassel near where it is sewn. Trim tassel.

If you enlarge the design for a bell pull or a guitar strap you may want to work the leaves in a solid stitch such as Satin Stitch (59). Make it the required length and finish without the pointed end.

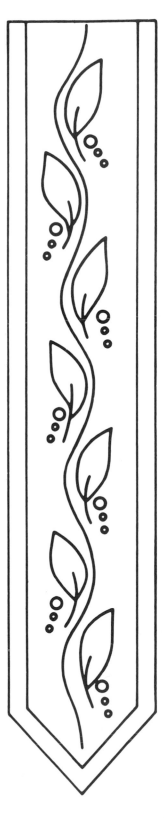

Diagram for Twining Vine
Bookmark (actual size).

Decorative Mirror

Color photograph, following page 92

Here's a small-size mirror to hang in the kitchen, or to give as a gift. The design is so simple that it can easily be enlarged.

[Mirror]

Size:
6¾" x 9¾"

Materials:
12" x 15" piece of violet handwoven cotton, homespun-type cotton or linen
Crewel wool, one 30-yard card each: red, magenta and orange
Violet sewing thread
6¾" x 9¾" piece of mirror
Masking tape
Glue-on picture hanger

Pattern:
Trace diagram on page 84 (one half shown actual size). Complete other half of pattern by reversing design. Transfer to background fabric.

Working Method:
Place work in an embroidery hoop. Follow alphabetical key on diagram for colors. Use two strands of wool throughout. Work all lines in Holbein Stitch (45), all dots in French Knots (42). Work center of round motif in straight Roman Stitches (56) alternated with small Straight Stitches (70). (Numbers refer to stitches listed in Glossary, page 29.)

Finishing:
Trim embroidered piece to 9¾" x 12¾". Cut oval from center of fabric, leaving ¼" allowance inside the embroidered lines. Turn under allowance and sew in place so that

stitches don't show. Bind outside edges of mirror with masking tape to keep them from cutting the fabric. Block embroidered piece. Center on mirror, draw extra fabric to back and fasten with masking tape. Attach a glue-on hanger on the back.

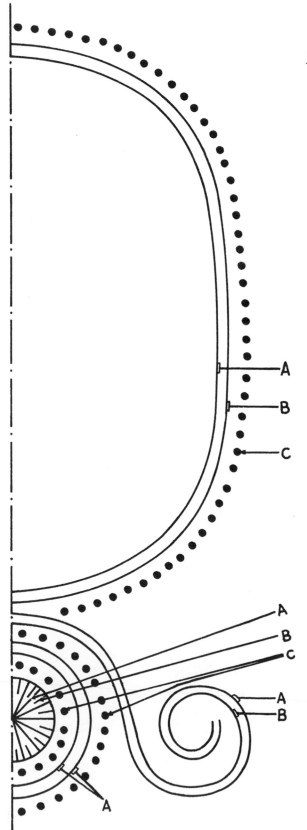

Diagram for Decorative Mirror
(one half shown, actual size).

Color Key:
A. *Red*
B. *Magenta*
C. *Orange*
— *Work narrow line*

Two Butterfly Designs

Color photograph, following page 92

These little butterflies were designed to add bright spots of color almost anywhere. Mounted on easels they will add a gay note to a coffee table or an end table. As wall hangings they will spark up a dark area in the hall or foyer or decorate the wall of a little girl's room. These motifs lend themselves to all kinds of embroidery uses. Apply one to a sweater or the bib of an apron. Scatter a few on café curtains for the breakfast room. Or reduce the size slightly and use them for coasters or as covers for inexpensive metal bookends. (Remember to use cotton thread on articles that require frequent washing.)

[Butterfly Plaque #1]

Size:
4¼″ x 4¾″

Materials:
8¼″ x 8¾″ piece blue homespun-type cotton
Crewel wool, one 30-yard card each: golden brown and black; a few yards each: medium blue, light blue, red and peach
4¼″ x 4¾″ piece of stiff cardboard
Masking tape

Pattern:
Trace diagram on page 87 (one half of butterfly is shown actual size). Complete other half of pattern by reversing design. Transfer to background fabric.

Working Method:
Place work in a hoop. Use two strands of wool throughout unless otherwise indicated. Using Satin Stitch (59), work vertical bands of color on wings and work body following color indicated on diagram. Work peach and black areas at

outer edge of upper wings in Chain Stitch (13). Work dots in French Knots (42). With one strand of black, work all horizontal lines on wings in Split Stitch (67). Also work "feelers" and around outer edges in Split Stitch with one strand of black. (Numbers refer to stitches listed in Glossary, page 29.)

Finishing:
Trim embroidered piece to 6¼" x 6¾". Block and finish following directions for Making a Wall Panel (page 155).

[Butterfly Plaque #2]
Color photograph, following page 92

Size:
4¼" x 4¾"

Materials:
8¼" x 8¾" piece of yellow homespun-type cotton
Crewel wool, a few yards each: purple, turquoise, pale green, kelly green, olive and shocking pink
4¼" x 4¾" piece of stiff cardboard
Masking tape

Pattern:
Trace and transfer as for Butterfly #1.

Working Method:
Place work in a hoop. Use two strands of wool throughout. Work body and wings in Split Stitch (67) worked in close rows, following diagram for colors. Dots are French Knots (42). (Numbers refer to stitches listed in Glossary, page 29.) The three dots on each turquoise spot on the wings should be in shocking pink French Knots.

Finishing:
Block and finish as for Butterfly #1.

Diagram for Butterfly #1
(one half shown, actual size).

Color Key:
A. *Golden Brown*
B. *Medium Blue*
C. *Light Blue*
D. *Red*
E. *Peach*
F. *Black*

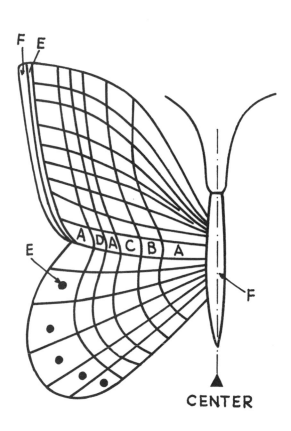

Diagram for Butterfly #2
(one half shown, actual size).

Color Key:
A. *Purple*
B. *Turquoise*
C. *Pale Green*
D. *Kelly Green*
E. *Olive*
F. *Shocking Pink*

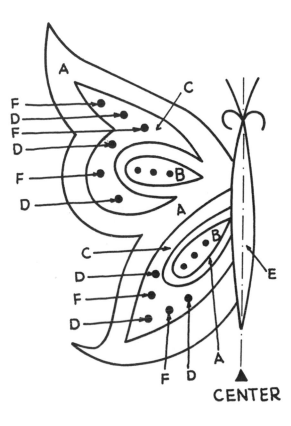

Two Small Motifs for Embroidery – Flying Bird, Walking Bird

Color photograph, following page 92

When you are in an embroidering mood, it is nice to have a few small, versatile motifs ready to use. These cheerful birds will lend themselves to almost anything your imagination can cook up. Try them on children's clothes, or put one on the pocket of a summer dress for you. Use one to decorate an address book cover or, most appropriately, a birdcage cover. Or why not mount them for plaques in a kitchen?

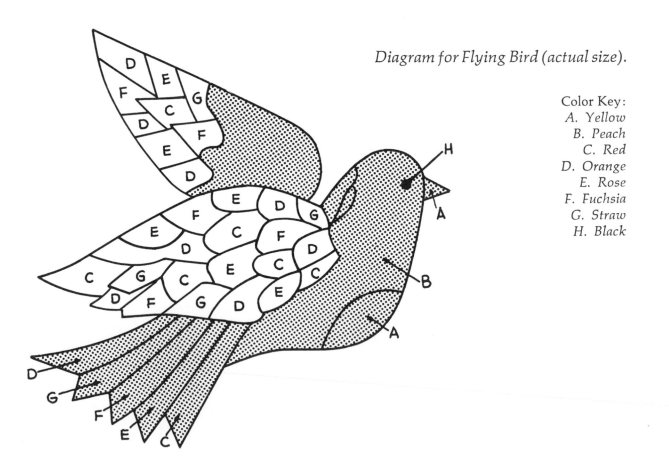

Diagram for Flying Bird (actual size).

Color Key:
A. *Yellow*
B. *Peach*
C. *Red*
D. *Orange*
E. *Rose*
F. *Fuchsia*
G. *Straw*
H. *Black*

[Flying Bird Plaque]

Size:
5″ square

Materials:
9″ square of blue homespun-type cotton
Crewel wool, a few yards each: yellow, peach, red, orange,
   rose, fuchsia, straw and black
5″ square piece of stiff cardboard
Masking tape

Pattern:
Trace diagram (shown actual size) and transfer to background fabric.

Working Method:
Place work in a hoop. Use two strands of wool throughout.
Shaded areas in diagram are worked in Split Stitch (67), un-
shaded areas in Satin Stitch (59). (Numbers refer to stitches
listed in Glossary, page 29.) Eye is worked in Satin Stitch,
too. Follow alphabetical key on diagram for colors.

Finishing:
Trim embroidered piece to 7″ square. Block and finish following directions for Making a Wall Panel (page 155).

[Walking Bird Plaque]

Size:
6″ square

Materials:
10″ square of bright pink homespun-type cotton
Crewel wool, one 30-yard card of lavender and a few yards
   each: shocking pink, magenta and pale green
6″ square of stiff cardboard
Masking tape

Pattern:
Trace diagram (shown actual size) and transfer to background fabric.

Working Method:
Place work in a hoop. Follow alphabetical key on diagram for colors. Using two strands and starting at center of wing, fill areas in Split Stitch (67). Work body in Chain Stitch (13), tail feathers in Split Stitch. Outline wing and tail feathers in a single strand, using Split Stitch. Using two strands, work four French Knots (42) for eye. Using a single strand, work legs and feet in Chain Stitch, beak in Split Stitch. (Numbers refer to stitches listed in Glossary, page 29.)

Finishing:
Trim embroidered piece to 8″ square. Block and finish as for Flying Bird.

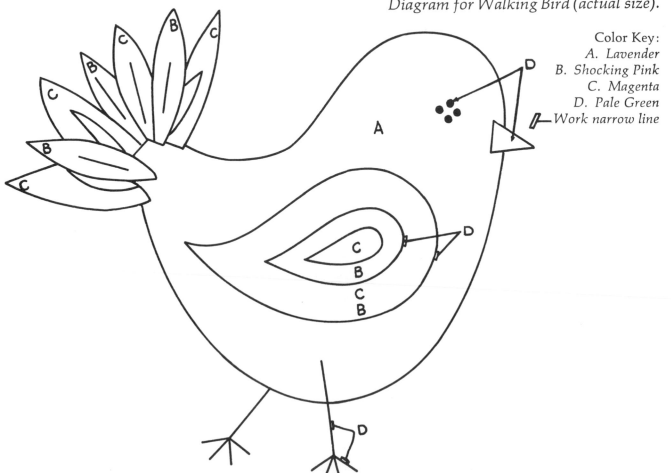

Diagram for Walking Bird (actual size).

Color Key:
A. *Lavender*
B. *Shocking Pink*
C. *Magenta*
D. *Pale Green*
Work narrow line

Whirling Wheels Pillow

Color photograph, following page 92

This simple design of whirling wheels will help you perfect your Chain Stitches and French Knots. You might even want to try a second pillow using other stitches such as Coral Stitch or Holbein Stitch. The design lends itself very well to other uses, perhaps a tote or shoulder bag. Or adapted to the right shape, it would make an attractive tennis racket cover or chair seat.

[Pillow]

Size:
14" square

Materials:
Two 18" squares of heavy cotton, one black, one golden brown
Knitting worsted, one small skein of each: golden brown, sand, pink and taupe
Black and white sewing thread
Two 15" squares of muslin
Stuffing material

Pattern:
Enlarge diagram on page 92 (each small square=1" square).
Transfer to black background fabric.

Working Method:
Place work in an embroidery hoop. Use one strand of wool throughout. Following colors on diagram, work wheel centers in Straight Stitch (70). Dots in diagram are French Knots (42); broken lines are Chain Stitch (13). (Numbers refer to stitches listed in Glossary, page 29.) Work solid lines in Chain Stitch then tie down each chain with a little Straight Stitch over each side of the loop.

Finishing:
Block then trim embroidered piece to 15″ square (includes
½″ seam allowance all around). Cut brown square same size
for pillow back. Finish pillow following directions for Making a Pillow (page 151).

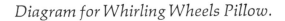

Diagram for Whirling Wheels Pillow.

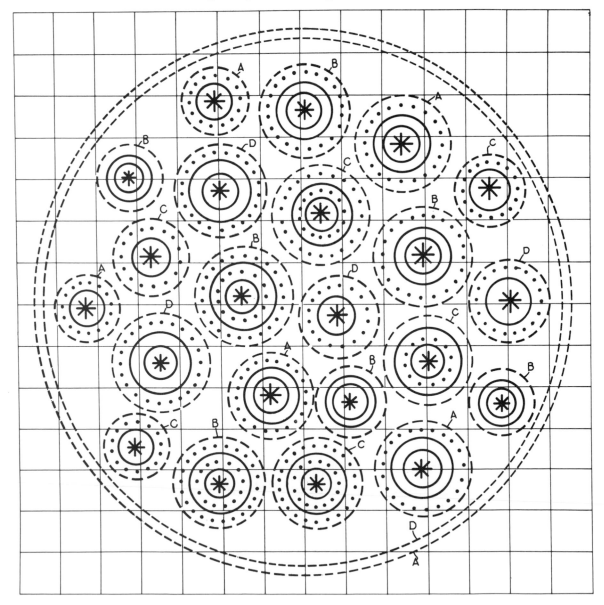

Color Key: *A. Golden Brown; B. Sand; C. Pink; D. Taupe*

(Clockwise) Bird and Tulip Pillow (p. 111); Whirling Wheels Pillow (p. 91); Antique Floral Pillow (p. 120); Paisley Pillow (p. 100); Ascension Balloon Pillow (p. 108); Calico Cat Cushion (p. 115).

Two Butterfly Designs (p. 85); Flying Bird (p. 88); Walking Bird (p. 90); Summer Handbag (p. 127); Decorative Mirror (p. 82).

Singapore Bird Chair Seat (p. 144).

Classic Tote Bag (p. 98); Graphic Wall Hanging (p. 130).

Winter Wonderland

Although no snow-covered fields or frozen rivulets are visible in this wall panel, it is reminiscent of the frosty feeling of a January afternoon. The cold blues and fluffy whites bring to mind any number of winter scenes.

Limited to four basic stitches, this design can be used in a number of different ways. It makes an interesting wall panel. Or it could be framed, made up into a pillow, a tote bag, or a book cover.

[Wall Panel]

Size:
10" x 14½"

Materials:
16" x 20½" piece of natural-color linen or cotton
Crewel wool, one 30-yard card each: light blue, medium blue, dark blue, light gray, dark gray and beige
A few yards each: smooth white nylon baby yarn and white mohair or angora yarn
10" x 14½" piece of heavy cardboard
Masking tape

Pattern:
Enlarge diagram on page 95 (each small square=½" square). Transfer to background fabric.

Working Method:
Place work in an embroidery hoop. Use two strands of all yarns except mohair which should be used in a single strand. First work all straight lines in Outline Stitch (53), Split Stitch (67) and Chain Stitch (13), using them at will on the lines. (Numbers refer to stitches listed in Glossary, page 29.) Also make a random use of all colors over the design, making a pleasing relationship of one color to another. Work dots in French Knots (42), using all yarns except mohair.

Finishing:

Block, then trim embroidered piece to 14″ x 18½″. Mount following directions for Making a Wall Panel (page 155).

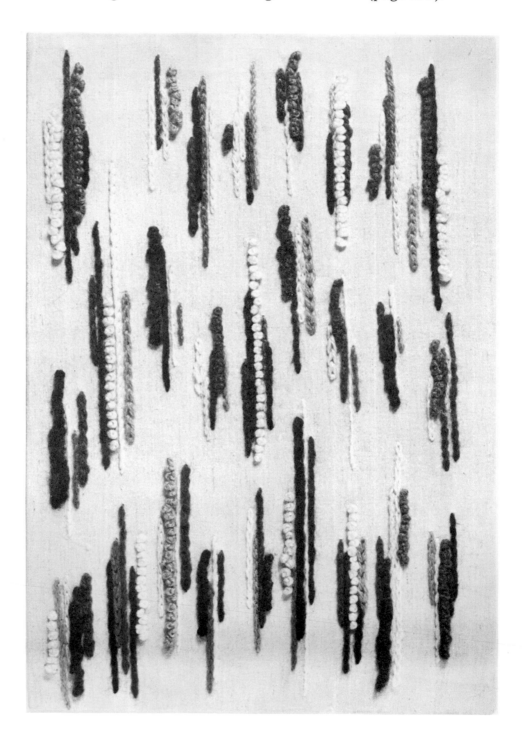

Diagram for Winter Wonderland Wall Panel.

7. Projects for Needleworkers with Some Experience

Accent Crewel

Occasionally an embroiderer who has some skill with a needle prefers not to set up her own designs. Here is a creative way to use beautiful designs without enlarging and transferring patterns. Just choose a printed fabric you like and use part of its design for your embroidery. It can be as simple as a plain striped or checked fabric or as lavish as an elaborate print. Be sure that the background fabric is a suitable weave for embroidery (see Fabrics, page 16).

You can use this method for a little throw pillow, a wingback chair or a room full of draperies. One embroiderer used this method to embellish a drapery for a picture window. The upper sections of the drapery were worked, then the draperies were hung at the window for the family to enjoy. The lower sections were worked later right at the window!

Although most stitches can be used on prints, it is wise not to use ones that are so elaborate that they conflict with the pattern of the fabric itself. They should be selected to enhance the lines, the colors or particular areas of the pattern. Generally it would be too time-consuming to do solid stitchery on an entire piece unless it were quite small.

A good way to try this technique would be to make a pillow cover of ½ yard of fabric with a clear print design. Run a basting thread around an area just the size of a pillow (12″ or 14″ square or round).

Now get out your yarns and choose a few that will blend or contrast with the colors of the print. Some can be shiny, others can have a matte finish. Lay a length or two of yarn as an outline on some of the lines of the design. Snip off a few ¼″ pieces of yarn and place them on the design. This will give you an idea of the effect you want to achieve. Choose stitches that will give this effect—and plunge right in.

On the other hand, you may have a handsome printed wool, silk or linen dress that will look simply smashing with this sort of embroidery. If you make your own clothes, of course, you can start from scratch. But wonderful effects can be achieved on ready-made clothes. You probably won't want to embroider an entire garment, but just think what some stitchery will add to the neckline of a dress or the cuffs of a printed jersey blouse or even the bottom of the pants of hostess pajamas.

To work on garments, fold back hems, facings or linings and work only on the garment itself if possible. Be sure to handle the garment carefully in your embroidery hoop so the fabric is not stretched.

The piece shown, known as "Pheasants and Quail," was worked in Satin Stitch (59) on a few solid areas of the design, Outline Stitch (53) on the reeds and Seed Stitch (63) to give texture to some of the other areas of dense color. (Numbers refer to stitches listed in Glossary, page 29.)

Whatever you try, you may find this technique so fascinating that you will have trouble leaving a printed fabric unadorned.

Section of printed fabric accented with crewel embroidery.

Classic Tote Bag

Color photograph, following page 92

No matter how heavy your bundles may be, carrying them in this commodious tote will lighten the burden. The design, embroidered in just three simple stitches, is so adaptable that it could be made into a pillow, a footstool or an interesting wall hanging.

[Tote Bag]

Size:
13½″ square

Materials:
Heavy cotton, one 18″ square of natural color and 1 yard 36″-wide red orange
Two 14½″ squares interfacing
Crewel yarn, one 30-yard card each black and golden brown
Sewing thread

Pattern:
Enlarge diagram on page 99 for one quarter of pattern (each small square = ½″ square). Complete pattern by repeating around a center then transfer to natural-color square.

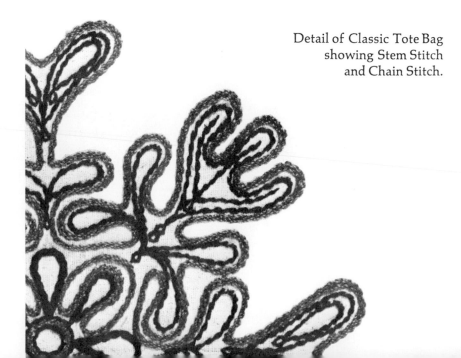

Detail of Classic Tote Bag showing Stem Stitch and Chain Stitch.

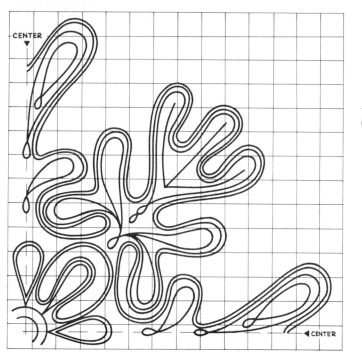

Diagram for
Classic Tote Bag.

Working Method:

Place work in an embroidery hoop or frame. Use two strands of wool throughout. Work two center rings in Stem Stitch (69) in black. Between them work a ring of brown Chain Stitch (13). (Numbers refer to stitches listed in Glossary, page 29.) Work all units that touch center rings in black Stem Stitch. Shapes that fit into these are worked in brown Stem Stitch. Work all double outer lines of pattern in brown Stem Stitch. Work all remaining lines in black Stem Stitch except small loops on pattern. Work these in black Lazy-Daisy Stitch (50), catching each Lazy-Daisy at the sides as well as the bottom of the loop with a small stitch to round it out. If you wish, other line stitches such as Holbein (45) or Backstitch (2) can replace the Stem Stitch or Chain Stitch.

Finishing:

Block the embroidered piece. Cut embroidered piece 14½" square, and one piece of orange fabric 14½" square. For lining, cut two 14½" squares of orange. For handles, cut two pieces of orange each 2½" x 13".

Finish following directions for How to Make a Tote Bag (page 156).

Paisley Pillow

Color photograph, following page 92

If you took the blobs of rich color on an artist's palette and swirled them into a bold paisley design, you'd come up with the plan for this colorful sofa pillow. Although it is worked with fairly solid embroidery, the heavy yarn and large stitches make it go rather quickly. In fact, if you repeat the design to the necessary length, it could be used as a fabulous border for an evening skirt. Or it could be developed into an allover pattern for a vest.

This is an excellent choice if you have had only limited needlework experience since the large stitches do not require great skill to give a satisfactory effect.

Detail of Paisley Pillow showing great variety of stitches.

[Pillow]

Size:
11" x 16½"

Materials:
5/8 yard white homespun-type cotton
Knitting worsted, a few yards each: pink, rose, shocking
    pink, scarlet, yellow, gold, apricot, orange, light green,
    green, olive, light blue, medium blue, royal, turquoise,
    plum and brown
White sewing thread
Two 12" x 17½" pieces of muslin
Stuffing material

Pattern:
Enlarge diagram on page 102 (each small square = ½"
square). Transfer to background fabric cut 17" x 22½".

Working Method:
Place work in an embroidery frame. No colors are indicated on the diagram since the wide variety would make
the diagram too difficult to follow. Just use one strand of
yarn in the colors desired or follow the color photograph.
Work all lines in Outline Stitch (53) unless otherwise indicated. Work star-shaped units in Star Filling Stitch (68),
dots in French Knots (42). Where Cross-Stitch (32) and
Trellis Stitch (72) are indicated, tie at center with a little
stitch. (Numbers refer to stitches listed in Glossary, page
29.) Work all other stitches following the numbers on the
diagram.

Finishing:
Trim embroidered piece to 12" x 17½" (includes ½" seam
allowance all around). Cut a similar piece for backing.
Block and finish following directions for Making a Pillow
(page 151).

Diagram for Paisley Pillow.

Fanciful Fish Picture

Color photograph, following page 116

Since this design includes only six basic stitches, it is a fine project to start after you have made a few simple pieces and are ready to tackle a little more ambitious work. If you prefer, the fish motif could be used on a pillow, a tote bag or on a felt skirt for a round table.

[Picture]

Size:
Circle 14″ in diameter

Materials:
18″ square of natural-color linen, rayon or cotton
Crewel yarn, one 30-yard card each: purple, kelly green, blue, navy, mauve, plum, rust, olive and light olive
Circle of heavy cardboard 14″ in diameter
Circle of ¼″-thick foam rubber 14″ in diameter
White glue
Masking tape
Round picture frame with opening 14″ in diameter

Pattern:
Enlarge diagram on page 105 (each small square = ½″ square). Transfer to background fabric.

Working Method:
Place work in an embroidery frame or hoop. Use a single strand of wool throughout, except use a double strand for French Knots (42). Follow alphabetical key on diagram for colors. The Straight Stitches (70) on center of fish are indicated by three lines; however, work from five to ten Straight Stitches on each scale to fill the space well. (Numbers refer to stitches listed in Glossary, page 29). Carry some of kelly green around eye area down into blue area of snout.

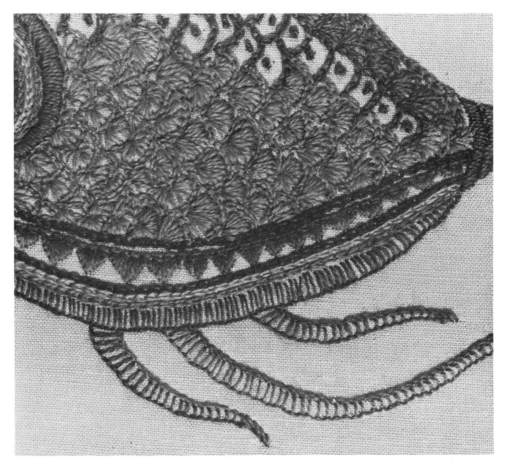

Detail of Fanciful Fish Picture showing Straight Stitch, Blanket Stitch and others.

Finishing:
Block, then trim embroidered piece to an 18″ circle. Finish following directions for Framing a Picture (page 153). NOTE: The fish pictured in the illustration (following page 116) has olive-green velvet tubing glued around the inner edge of the frame for a neat finish.

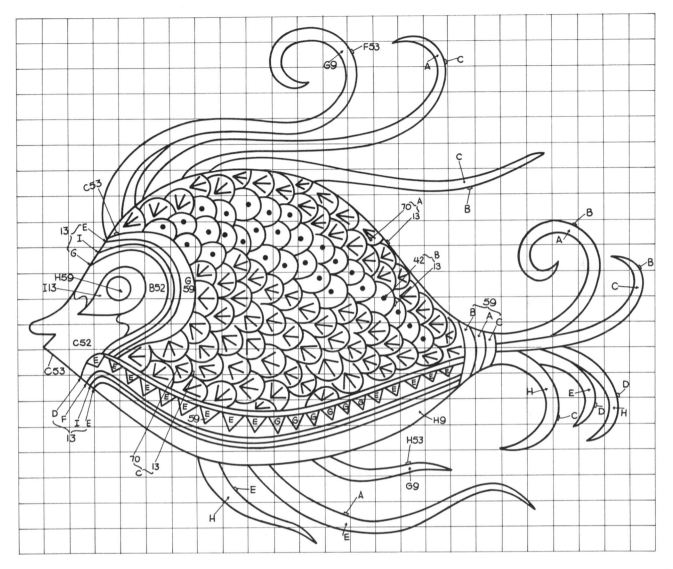

Diagram for Fanciful Fish Picture.

Color Key:
A. Purple
B. Kelly Green
C. Blue
D. Navy
E. Mauve
F. Plum
G. Rust
H. Olive
I. Light Olive
⬦——— Work narrow line
Numbers refer to stitches listed in glossary

8. Projects for More Experienced Needleworkers

Abstract Picture

Color photograph, following page 116

For those with a modern turn of mind here's a design that will give you the chance to use a variety of unusual stitches—Honeycomb Filling and Cloud Filling, Spider Web and Double Herringbone. The design also lends itself to a variety of uses. Try it on a telephone book cover or a photo album, a pillow or a knitting bag.

[Picture]

Size:
10" x 12"

Materials:
16" x 18" piece of natural-color raw silk or linen
Crewel yarn, one 30-yard card each: yellow, light green, medium green, tan, brown, rust and henna
10" x 12" piece of heavy cardboard
10" x 12" piece of ¼"-thick foam rubber
White glue
Masking tape
Picture frame with a 10" x 12" opening

Pattern:
Enlarge diagram on page 107 (each small square = ½" square). Transfer to background fabric.

Working Method:
Place work in a hoop. Start embroidery at center and continue out to sides of design following the alphabetical key on diagram for colors. To do the Double Herringbone Stitch

work the area indicated for Herringbone Stitch (43). Then
go back over the area in the second color, making a stitch
between each two on previous row and weaving under the
previous stitches. To work Cloud Filling Stitch (24), make
the little stitches in henna, then work the next step in light
green. (Numbers refer to stitches listed in Glossary, page 29.)

Finishing:

Block, then trim embroidered piece to 13" x 15". Finish following directions for Framing a Picture (page 153).

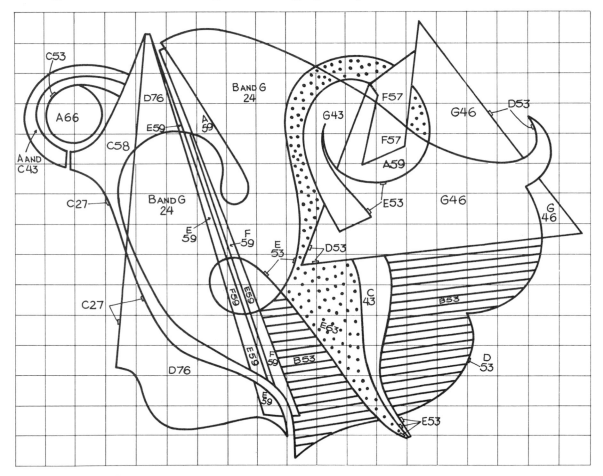

Diagram for Abstract Picture.

Color Key:

A. Yellow	E. Brown
B. Light Green	F. Rust
C. Medium Green	G. Henna
D. Tan	⌿——— Work narrow line

Numbers refer to stitches listed in glossary

Ascension Balloon Pillow

Color photograph, following page 92

Try this design when you feel confident enough to tackle a piece that's fun and not too difficult but does require neat fine stitchery. There is enough variety in the stitches to make the work interesting. If the design appeals to you but you don't need a pillow, you might make this for a tray and place it under glass. Or frame it for a picture.

[Pillow]

Size:
Circle 14″ in diameter

Materials:
½ yard 36″-wide natural-color linen
Crewel yarn, one 30-yard card each: rose, light blue, bright blue, violet, acid green, light brown, dark brown and yellow
White sewing thread
Two circles of muslin 15″ in diameter
Stuffing material
1½ yards bright blue twisted cotton cord

Pattern:
Enlarge diagram on page 110 (each small square = ½″ square). Transfer to background fabric cut 18″ square.

Working Method:
Place work in a hoop. Follow alphabetical key on diagram for colors. In all shaded areas work Satin Stitch (59). Use a single strand throughout, except use a double strand on the Laid Stitch (48) and Running Stitch (58) of the basket. To embroider basket, make one long Laid Stitch on all vertical lines. Weave across them with Running Stitch on the horizontal lines. The four long shroud lines (broken lines in diagram) each consist of a long Laid Stitch. They were de-

signed to give a realistic effect. Although these may break with use, they are easily replaced. If you prefer, they may be worked in Outline Stitch (53). (Numbers refer to stitches listed in Glossary, page 29.)

Finishing:
Block, then trim embroidered piece to circle with a 15″ diameter (includes ½″ seam allowance all around). Cut a similar piece for pillow back. Finish following directions for Making a Pillow (page 151). Sew cord around seam.

Detail of Ascension Balloon Pillow showing the long shroud lines in Laid Stitch.

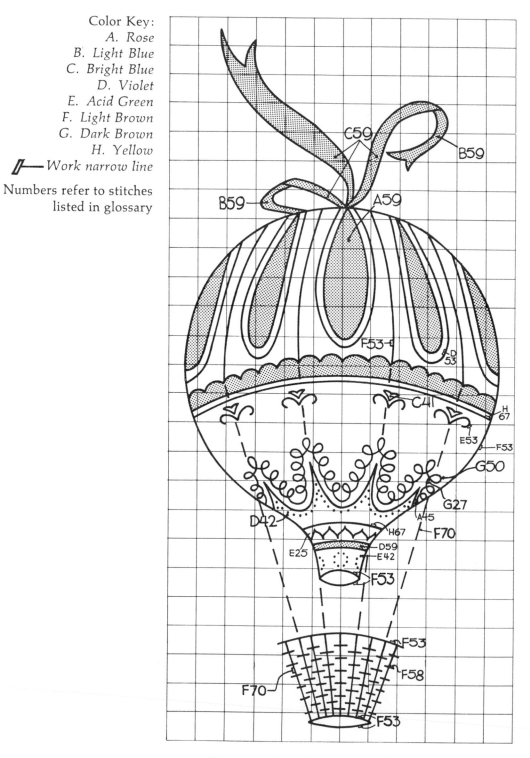

Color Key:
A. Rose
B. Light Blue
C. Bright Blue
D. Violet
E. Acid Green
F. Light Brown
G. Dark Brown
H. Yellow
—Work narrow line

Numbers refer to stitches
listed in glossary

Diagram for Ascension Balloon Pillow.

Bird and Tulip Pillow

Color photograph, following page 92

Strong peasant colors and the favorite bird and flower motifs of the Pennsylvania Dutch produce a pillow that would be as welcome in a city apartment as in a country home. Although the design can be developed in your own choice of stitches, you may find it interesting to use the Holbein and Coral Stitches which were used on the actual pillow. The various parts of the design are also adaptable to a number of other applications. The bird (worked in cotton) could embellish a child's dress; a tulip might decorate a lingerie case or a notebook.

[Pillow]

Size:
15" square

Materials:
½ yard natural-color linen or cotton
Crewel yarn, one 30-yard card each: green, olive, teal, turquoise, maroon, blue, burnt orange, violet, rose, red and magenta
Two 16" squares muslin
White sewing thread
Stuffing material

Pattern:
Enlarge diagram on page 113 (each small square = 1" square). Transfer to linen or cotton background fabric cut to 18" square.

Working Method:
Place work in an embroidery hoop or frame. Use two strands of wool throughout. Follow alphabetical key on diagram for colors. All stems are Holbein Stitch (45). All leaves are Hol-

bein Stitch except that the second line from the outside of all leaves is always Coral Stitch (25). The center of all flowers is worked in solid Holbein Stitch. After the bird is worked, fill in the body with scattered blue French Knots (42), and the head with scattered maroon French Knots. An alternate method would be to work Backstitch (2) or Outline Stitch (53) instead of the Holbein throughout. Or you could use Couching Stitch (27) or Scroll Stitch (62) wherever Coral Stitch was used. (Numbers refer to stitches listed in Glossary, page 29.)

Finishing:
Block, then trim embroidered piece to 16″ square (includes ½″ seam allowance all around). Cut a similar piece for pillow back. Finish following directions for Making a Pillow (page 151).

Diagram for Bird and Tulip Pillow.

Color Key:
A. Green
B. Olive
C. Teal
D. Turquoise
E. Maroon
F. Blue
G. Burnt Orange
H. Violet
I. Rose
J. Red
K. Magenta
⟋——Work narrow line

Numbers refer to stitches listed in glossary

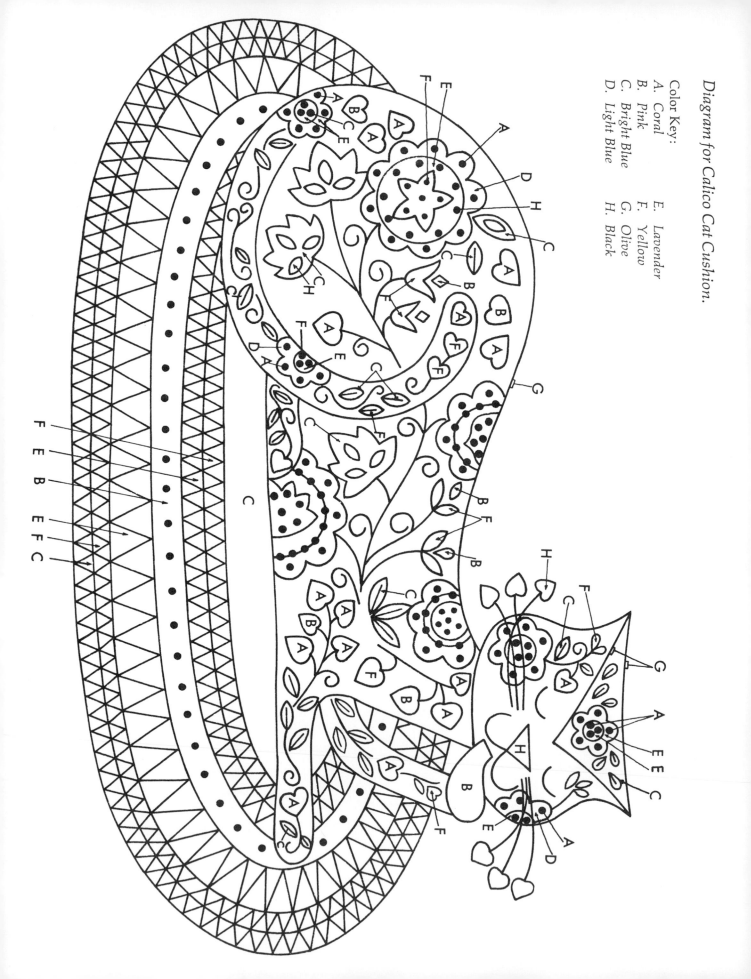

Diagram for Calico Cat Cushion.

Color Key:
A. Coral   E. Lavender
B. Pink   F. Yellow
C. Bright Blue   G. Olive
D. Light Blue   H. Black

Calico Cat Cushion

Color photograph, following page 92

The kettle is steaming on the hearth, chestnuts are roasting in the coals and the cat is contentedly cleaning his paws near the crackling fire. All the good sounds and smells and sights of a winter's evening in the country are captured in this little cushion. If you want a project to challenge your new-found skills, this is for you.

No need to limit the Calico Cat to a cushion. He might also make a nice flat pad for a captain's chair. Or he'd be cozy on a little foot-stool. And he could certainly be framed if you like.

[Cushion]

Size:
8½" x 13" oval

Materials:
⅜ yard chartreuse homespun-type cotton
Crewel yarn, one 30-yard card each: coral, pink, bright blue,
   light blue, lavender, yellow, olive and black
Black, chartreuse and white sewing thread
⅜ yard muslin
Stuffing material
1½ yards yellow twisted cotton cord

Pattern:
Trace diagram (actual size) for pattern. Transfer to 12½" x 17" piece of homespun.

Working Method:
Place work in hoop. Use one strand of wool throughout. Work bands on rug in close rows of Chain Stitch (13), area directly under cat in close rows of Stem Stitch (69). Work all decorative lines on cat in black Stem Stitch, all flowers, hearts and large leaves in Satin Stitch (59). Work little oval leaves and any oval shapes in Lazy-Daisy Stitch (50). Work

Detail of Calico Cat Cushion showing close rows of Chain Stitch for braided rug effect with superimposed Straight Stitches.

all dots in French Knots (42). These are always worked on top of Satin Stitch or Chain Stitch embroidery which is completed first. Cat's tongue is made up of close rows of Stem Stitch. To simulate the stitching on braided rug, use black sewing thread and work lines in Straight Stitch (70) when Chain Stitch is complete. (Numbers refer to stitches listed in Glossary, page 29.)

Finishing:
Block, then trim embroidered piece to 9½" x 14" oval (includes ½" seam allowances all around). Cut similar piece for back of cushion and two matching muslin pieces. Finish following directions for Making a Pillow (page 151). Sew cord around edge of cushion.

Proud Rooster Picture (p. 133).

(Clockwise) Garden of Flowers Picture (p. 137); Fanciful Fish Picture (p. 103).
Abstract Picture (p. 106); Zinneas and Asters Picture (p. 117).

(*Top*) Springtime Seat Cushion (p. 139); (*bottom*) Autumn Seat Cushion (p. 142).

Panel for Ecclesiastical Garment (p. 147).

Zinnias and Asters Picture

Color photograph, following page 116

The sweet spicy scent of garden flowers, the soft touch of a warm breeze and the rustle of leaves are caught in this picture that epitomizes a summer afternoon. Although the stitches are fairly basic ones, they are often used giant size, making this picture quick to make and interesting to embroider.

[Picture]

Size:
12" x 16"

Materials:
½ yard chartreuse homespun-type cotton
Crewel yarn, one 30-yard card each: yellow orange, orange, rose, red, green, white and bronze
12" x 16" piece of heavy cardboard
12" x 16" piece of ¼"-thick foam rubber.
Masking tape
White glue
Picture frame with a 12" x 16" opening

Pattern:
Enlarge diagram on page 119 (each small square=1" square).
Transfer to background fabric cut 18" x 22".

Working Method:
Place fabric in an embroidery frame. Follow alphabetical key on diagram for colors. Embroider zinnias with two strands of wool. On orange zinnia, surround center with Straight Stitch (70). When doing Fly Stitch (41) on oval bud, be sure to make stitches close together.

Using one strand of wool, work asters from the outside in. Overlap a ring of smaller Lazy-Daisy Stitches (50) over the first ring of large Lazy-Daisy Stitches. Fill centers solidly with French Knots (42) made with two strands.

When you have completed the large white daisies, using a single strand of bronze, embroider the centers in about twelve Straight Stitches. The tiny white flowers are made with a single strand in Buttonhole Stitch (9) around a center point. Also work their stems and French Knots with a single strand.

To embroider jug, first do Satin Stitch (59) on handle in a single strand. Work rest of jug with two strands. Outline handle with white, then with bronze. Make another bronze line on the outside of handle. Work all shading lines on jug first in white, then in bronze. Embroider long Laid Stitches (48) the height of the jug, threading them under any of the shading lines they cross. (Numbers refer to stitches listed in Glossary, page 29.)

Finishing:
Block, then trim embroidery to 16" x 20". Finish following directions for Framing a Picture (page 153).

Diagram for Zinnias and Asters Picture.

Color Key:
A. *Yellow Orange*
B. *Orange*
C. *Rose*
D. *Red*
E. *Green*
F. *White*
G. *Bronze*
—*Work narrow line*

Numbers refer to stitches
listed in glossary

Antique Floral Pillow

Color photograph, following page 92

A treasure trove of little swatches of embroidery found in an antique shop served as the inspiration for this pillow. The designs are shown as separate units so that you can use them separately on the pocket of a blouse, for a pin cushion, or a coaster. Or use in combination— in a row at the bottom of an apron, or repeated on the blocks of an afghan. Or you might enjoy making a chubby pillow like this one.

[Pillow]

Size:
9½" x 13¾"

Materials:
½ yard 36"-wide white linen
Crewel yarn, one 30-yard card each: violet, lavender, rose, yellow, gold, light green and dark green
½ yard 36"-wide muslin
White sewing thread
Stuffing material

Swatches of embroidery found in an antique shop. *Courtesy of Dorothy M. Sheehan.*

Detail of unit of Antique Floral Pillow (adapted from one of the swatches on opposite page) showing shading of Long and Short Stitch.

Pattern:

Trace diagrams on pages 122 and 123 (shown actual size) and set up with ½″ borders between them and ½″ border all around. Transfer to background fabric cut 13½″ x 17¾″.

Working Method:

Place work in an embroidery hoop or frame. Use one strand of yarn throughout. Follow alphabetical key on diagrams for colors. The main stitch requiring special mention is the Long and Short Stitch (52). Start at outer edge of petals with rose, then work lavender, then violet. Scatter a few yellow Seed Stitches (63) over violet area after it is worked. Also work centers of daisies in solid French Knots (42). When motifs are completed, make borders of Chevron Stitches (23) between motifs and all around outer edge of motifs. (Numbers refer to stitches listed in Glossary, page 29.)

Finishing:

Block, then trim embroidered piece to 10½″ x 14¾″ (including ½″ seam allowance all around). Cut a similar piece for pillow back and two matching muslin pieces. Finish following directions for Making a Pillow (page 151).

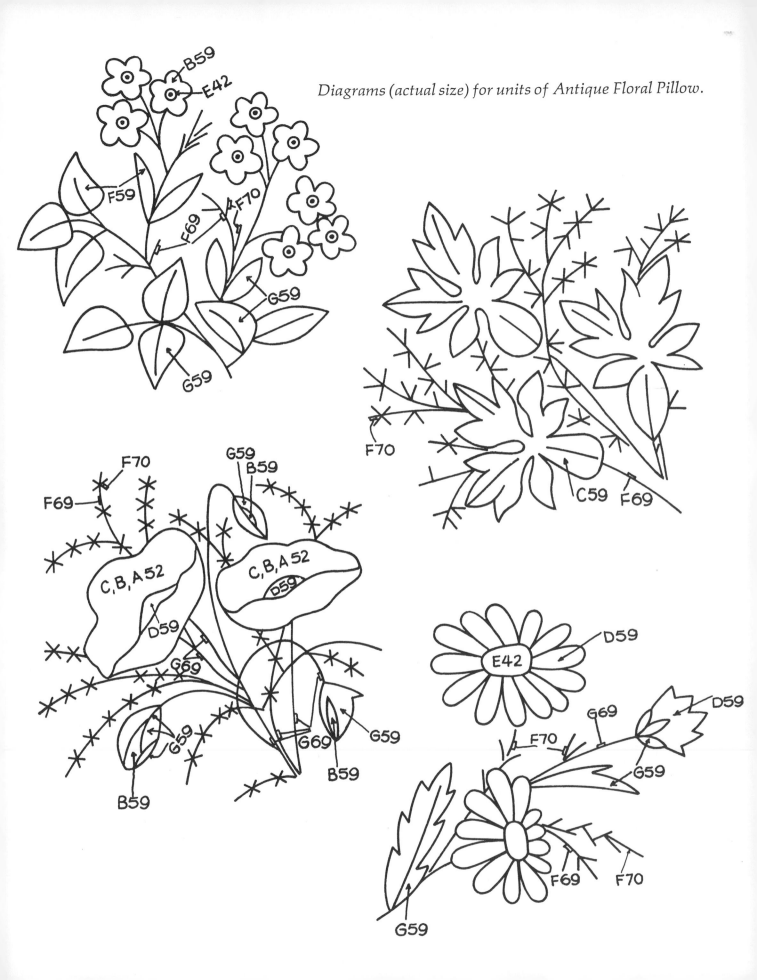

Diagrams (actual size) for units of Antique Floral Pillow.

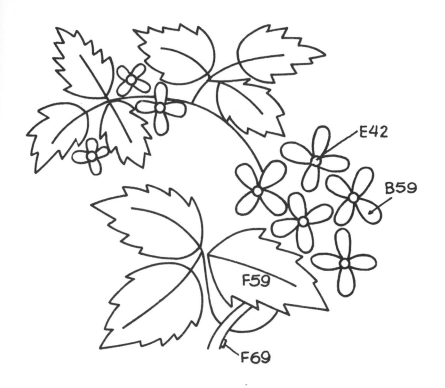

E42

B59

F59

F69

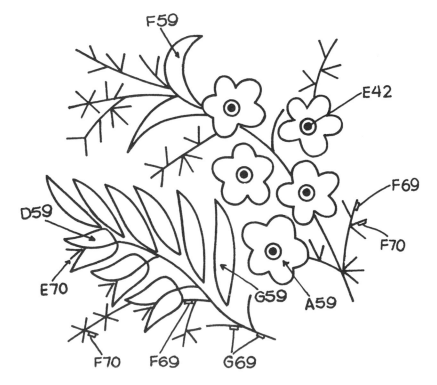

F59

E42

F69

F70

D59

E70

G59

A59

F70

F69

G69

Color Key:
A. *Violet*
B. *Lavender*
C. *Rose*
D. *Yellow*
E. *Gold*
F. *Light Green*
G. *Dark Green*
Work narrow line

Numbers refer to stitches
listed in glossary

Medusa Head Picture

Although the use of the human face and form is rare in the field of embroidery, it is not entirely unheard of, particularly in antique pieces. This modern version of the mythical Medusa head uses flowers, a bird and a butterfly in place of the traditional snakes. An improvement, don't you agree? The design would also make an attractive pillow.

[Picture]

Size:
Circle 16″ in diameter

Materials:
22″ square of white linen
Crewel wool, two 30-yard cards of bronze
Silk or rayon embroidery floss, one skein each: pink, rose, green, lavender, purple, yellow, beige, taupe, brown and black
Circle of heavy cardboard 16″ in diameter
Circle of ¼″-thick foam rubber 16″ in diameter
Masking tape
White glue
Round picture frame with opening 16″ in diameter

Pattern:
Enlarge diagram on page 126 (each small square = ½″ square). Transfer to background fabric.

Working Method:
Embroider entire head, face and hair (everything but shaded areas) in two strands of crewel wool, using Outline Stitch (53) throughout. Work shaded areas in three strands of silk.

Embroider bird in stripes of brown and beige Outline Stitch. Then work head and breast shading from rose to pink to beige Long and Short Stitch (52). Make yellow beak, rose crest, black chin area all in Satin Stitch (59). Make eye

Medusa Head Picture with flowers, a bird and a butterfly in the curving tresses.

in black French Knot (42) and foot in black Outline Stitch. (Numbers refer to stitches listed in Glossary, page 29.)

Embroider upper flower on left in pink shaded with a little rose Long and Short Stitch. Make leaf in green Satin Stitch.

Finishing:
Block, then trim embroidered piece to circle 19″ in diameter. Finish following directions for Framing a Picture (page 153).

Diagram for Medusa Head Picture.

9. Projects for Advanced Needleworkers

Summer Handbag

Color photograph, following page 92

Although crewel is not used on handbags as frequently as on tote bags, fine stitchery lends itself beautifully to both daytime and evening purses. This small handbag, with its delicate tracery of dainty stitches, would be a fascinating project.

The design offers many other possibilities . . . scattered on a white wool shawl, for example. If you're ambitious, you might even embroider a piece to cover the entire top of an end table and protect it with glass.

Detail of Summer Handbag showing variety of stitches used.

[Handbag]

Size:
8½" at widest part, 7" high without frame

Materials:
⅜ yard 36"-wide natural-color linen or silk
Crewel wool, one 30-yard card each: emerald, amethyst, dark green, turquoise, aquamarine and fuchsia
7"-wide handbag frame (one shown is an antique but frames may be purchased in some needlework or craft shops)
Sewing thread
⅜ yard nonwoven interfacing
⅜ yard 36"-wide lining fabric

Pattern:
Trace diagram (one half shown actual size). Complete other half of pattern by reversing design. Check to see if completed pattern fits your bag frame. If not, change the outline of pattern to fit. Transfer pattern to background fabric cut 13" x 14½". Make second piece exactly like the first for back of bag.

Working Method:
Place work in a hoop. Use one strand of wool throughout, except when indicated otherwise. Follow alphabetical key on diagram for colors. Note that outer section of large motif (marked A43) stops at dotted line. The upper line is then completed with Stem Stitch (69), from dotted line to end. Use two strands of wool for Bullion Stitches (8). (Numbers refer to stitches listed in Glossary, page 29). Embroider back of bag as you did the front.

Finishing:
Block the embroidered piece and finish following directions for How to Make a Handbag (page 156).

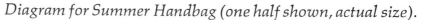

Diagram for Summer Handbag (one half shown, actual size).

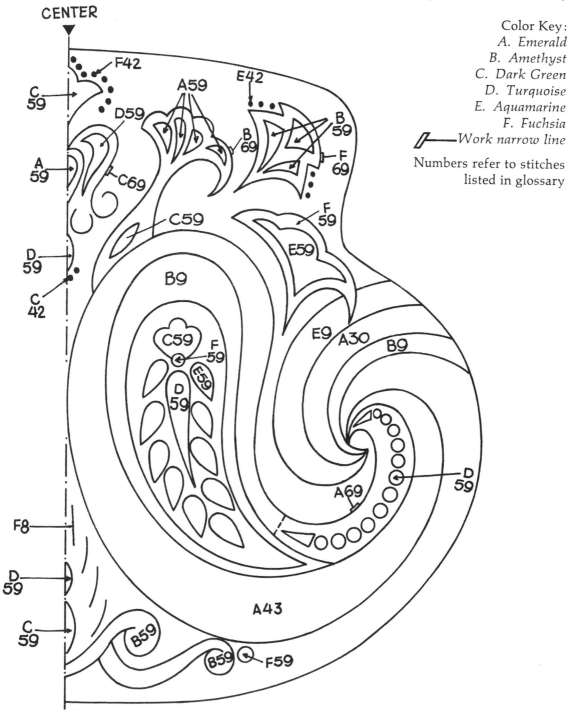

CENTER

Color Key:
A. *Emerald*
B. *Amethyst*
C. *Dark Green*
D. *Turquoise*
E. *Aquamarine*
F. *Fuchsia*
—Work narrow line

Numbers refer to stitches
listed in glossary

F42

C
59

A59

E42

D59

B
59

B
69

A
59

C69

F
69

C59

F
59

E59

D
59

B9

E9 A30 B9

C59

F
59

E59

D
59

C
42

F8

D
59

A69

D
59

D
59

A43

C
59

B59

B59 F59

Graphic Wall Hanging

Color photograph, following page 92

This example of modern graphics translates the old-time framed motto into today's idiom. And along with the uplifting words also comes a fine opportunity to work a great variety of interesting stitches—from Closed Feather Stitch to Bokhara Couching Stitch.

[Wall Hanging]

Size:
18″ x 26″

Materials:
24″ x 32″ piece of white linen
Assortment of wool yarns in various colors and weights
18″ x 26″ piece of heavy cardboard
18″ x 26″ piece of ¼″-thick foam rubber
Masking tape
White glue
Picture frame with 18″ x 26″ opening

Pattern:
Enlarge diagram on page 131 (each small square=1″ square). Transfer to background fabric.

Working Method:
Place piece in an embroidery frame. Work words as follows (colors are merely suggestions; numbers refer to stitches as listed in Glossary, page 29): Embroider *Beauty* in bright blue Closed Feather Stitch (35). *Duty* is turquoise Buttonhole Stitch (9). Work *Honesty* in lavender Chain Stitch (13). *Hope* is coral Bokhara Couching Stitch (28). *Faith* is fuchsia Herringbone Stitch (43), worked rather closely. Embroider *Humor* in amethyst Cloud Filling Stitch (24) with the little straight stitches worked in purple. Edge with purple Outline Stitch (53).

Diagram for Graphic Wall Hanging.

Work *Simplicity* in grass-green Satin Stitch (59) in the solid areas, Stem Stitch (69) on the lines. *Love* is turquoise Seed Stitch (63) with outlines in Stem Stitch (69). *Peace* is magenta Chain Stitch (13). Embroider *Humility* in bright blue Satin Stitch (59). *Charity* is worked in three rows of Holbein Stitch (45)—apple green, medium blue and apple green. *Liberty* is an outer row of Holbein Stitch (45), an inner row of French Knots (42) both in shocking pink. *Trust* is royal blue Satin Stitch (59). Do *Freedom* in yellow Open Chain Stitch (19). Try *Knowledge* in Holbein Stitch (45), alternating one letter of red and one of orange.

Finishing:

Block embroidered piece. Trim to 22″ x 30″. Mount and finish following directions for Framing a Picture (page 153). If you prefer, this embroidery may be finished as a wall hanging following directions on page 155.

Proud Rooster Picture

Color photograph, following page 116

The fine stitchery needed for the lifelike shading in this elegant rooster is a challenge even to the expert. The original was worked by a man with twenty years of needlework experience. Reproduce this handsome bird only if you are sure of your ability as a needleworker.

[Picture]

Size:
16" x 21"

Materials:
22" x 27" piece of natural-color linen
6-strand cotton embroidery floss in red, maroon, black, white, tan, light brown, dark brown, light yellow, medium yellow, gold, gray, orange, apple green, lime green, grass green, kelly green, aqua, light blue, medium blue, royal blue, indigo, magenta, fuchsia, scarlet, apricot and pink
16" x 21" piece of heavy cardboard
16" x 21" piece of ¼"-thick foam rubber
White glue
Masking tape
Picture frame with a 16" x 21" opening

Pattern:
Enlarge diagram on page 136 (each small square=1" square). Transfer to background fabric.

Working Method:
Place work in an embroidery frame. Use three strands of floss throughout, except for little black stitches on wing feathers use two strands. Refer to color photograph for colors. Edge all areas except tail feathers with Outline

Detail of Proud Rooster Picture showing lifelike shading of Long and Short Stitch.

Stitch (53). (Numbers refer to stitches listed in Glossary, page 29.)

Head: Work horizontal stripes in brown and black close rows of Outline Stitch. Work eye in black Satin Stitch (59) with a white spot. Surround eye with white Satin Stitch. Work scalloped trim on head in white Satin Stitch.

Beak: Work in orange Satin Stitch. Underline upper beak with tan Overcast Stitch (54).

Comb: Work in close vertical rows of Outline Stitch using red, scarlet and maroon.

Wattle: Work in close horizontal rows of Outline Stitch using red and maroon.

Breast and Neck: Shade feathers from tan down through light brown, then dark brown using Long and Short Stitch (52). Edge with medium yellow Outline Stitch. Work four to seven Straight Stitches (70), in black on inner area of each feather.

Body and Thigh: Work in dark brown Long and Short Stitch. Add feather effect later by working V's in black Straight Stitches. Outline areas in black.

Feet: Work in light brown Satin Stitch. Do scaly parts in light yellow Satin Stitch. On inner edges outline in black, outer edge in light yellow. Work nails and spur in gray.

Wing: Work all rows of feathers in Long and Short Stitch. Work top row in dark brown. Make cross lines in gray, then in black. Below each make a few short Straight Stitches in black. Work next row of feathers shading dark brown, black, gray, tan, dark brown, gray. Work next row of feathers shading tan, light brown, dark brown, gray, black. Work next two rows of feathers shading tan, light brown, dark brown, light yellow, medium yellow, gray. Work last row as previous row adding gold then tan before the gray. Outline all feathers with medium yellow. Work lines at tip of lowest row of feathers with black Straight Stitches. Repeat these on all wing feathers (not shown on diagram), making stitches about ⅛″ long. Work spine down each feather in maroon Outline Stitch.

Tail: Work feathers going from one band of color to another in rainbow fashion (see color photograph) and using Satin Stitch. Work spine down center of feathers in black Outline Stitch.

Finishing:
Block, then trim embroidered piece to 20″ x 25″. Finish following directions for Framing a Picture (page 153).

Detail of Proud Rooster Picture showing shading on tips of feathers.

Diagram for Proud Rooster Picture.

Garden of Flowers Picture

Color photograph, following page 116

Reminiscent of an old English garden, this picture is filled with dahlias, tulips and a few imaginary species. Whenever a design is as jam-packed with floral motifs as this one, it becomes a treasure trove for the needleworker. The separate units can be used on a pillow, album cover, café curtains, a vest or evening stole.

[Picture]

Size:
21" x 24"

Materials:
27" x 30" piece of smooth cream-colored wool
Knitting worsted, one small skein each: pale olive, light olive, medium olive, dark olive, chartreuse, yellow, gold, orange, lavender, purple and American beauty red
21" x 24" piece of heavy cardboard
21" x 24" piece of ¼"-thick foam rubber
Masking tape
White glue
Picture frame with 21" x 24" opening

Pattern:
Enlarge diagram on page 138 (each small square=1" square).
Transfer to background fabric.

Working Method:
Place work in an embroidery frame. Use one strand of wool throughout. Follow alphabetical key on diagram for colors. (Numbers refer to stitches listed in Glossary, page 29.)

Finishing:
Block embroidered piece. Trim to 25" x 28". Mount and finish following directions for Framing a Picture (page 153).

Diagram for Garden of Flowers Picture.

Color Key:
A. Pale Olive
B. Light Olive
C. Medium Olive
D. Dark Olive
E. Chartreuse
F. Yellow
G. Gold

H. Orange
I. Lavender
J. Purple
K. American Beauty
⬚——— Work narrow line

Numbers refer to stitches
listed in glossary

Seat Cushions

Color photograph, following page 116

Nature is reflected in a dozen delightful ways in this pair of seat cushions. One cushion is worked in tender spring shades, the other in the warm tones of autumn. Either is fascinating to embroider and will give you pleasure for years to come.

Of course, the designs can be adapted for pillows or wall hangings. The alert needleworker will also find many elements in these designs that can be used as decorative motifs. The autumn leaves would be effective scattered down the front of a simple wool dress. The mushrooms would be most cheerful on a toaster cover or an electric mixer cover. The acorns might decorate the pocket of a child's jumper, a pin cushion, or even covers for metal bookends. Just be sure to use cotton thread on any items that require frequent washing.

[Springtime Cushion]

Size:
14" from front to back; 16" across front edge; 13" across back edge.

Materials:
1½ yards 36"-wide natural-color linen
Crewel wool, one 30-yard card each: beige, rose, red, pale green, light green, medium green, dark green, yellow, light gold, gold and dark gold
Sewing thread
1 yard 36"-wide muslin
3½ yards fine cording or string
Stuffing material

Pattern:
Enlarge diagram on page 141 (each small square = ½" square). Make a paper pattern of your chair seat. Fit enlarged pattern into seat pattern. If the entire design does not con-

form with outline of the seat pattern, adjust individual elements of the design where necessary. Cut background fabric following seat pattern and allow 3" extra on all edges. Transfer design to fabric.

Working Method:
Place work in an embroidery frame or hoop. Use one strand of wool throughout. Follow alphabetical key on diagram for colors. Fern leaves and fronds are shaded from dark at the bottom to light at the top. Changes of letters on leaves and fronds indicate points at which the shades of yarn change. Note that two leaves are pale green throughout. Stem Stitch (69) is worked in close rows on fronds but opens out to an outline only at the upper end of fronds. Work Fly Stitch (41) very closely wherever it is used. When ladybug is finished, work dark green French Knots (42) on the back. (Numbers refer to stitches listed in Glossary, page 29.)

Finishing:
Block embroidered piece. Finish following directions for Making a Box Pillow (page 152). Narrow linen ties can be tacked to each side of back of cushion to hold it in place on the chair.

Detail of Springtime Seat Cushion showing fine stitchery on mushrooms and fern fronds.

Diagram for Springtime Seat Cushion.

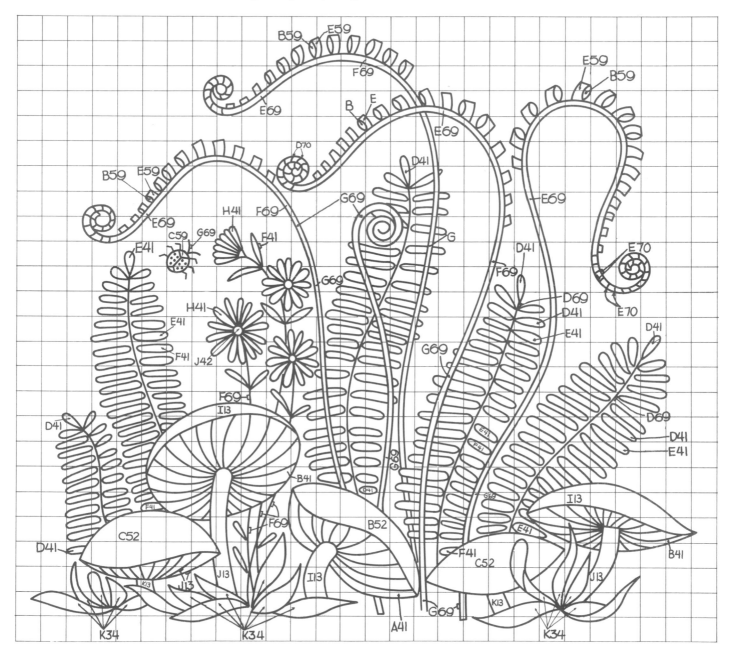

Color Key:
A. Beige
B. Rose
C. Red
D. Pale Green
E. Light Green
F. Medium Green
G. Dark Green
H. Yellow
I. Light Yellow
J. Gold
K. Dark Gold
⬚——— Work narrow line

Numbers refer to stitches listed in glossary

[Autumn Cushion]

Size:
Same as Springtime Cushion.

Materials:
Same as Springtime Cushion, except:
Crewel wool in beige, golden beige, apricot, pumpkin, yellow, gold, yellow orange, light golden brown, dark golden brown, light brown, medium brown, dark brown, bronze, light green, medium green, dark green

Pattern:
Enlarge diagram on page 143 and develop as for Springtime Cushion.

Working Method:
Follow general information for Springtime Cushion. Embroider goldenrod (shaded areas) in closely worked French Knots (42), mixing colors slightly from section to section. On graceful lines near oak leaves (marked L69 and 42) work Stem Stitch (69) then edge with scattered French Knots. For oak leaves shade colors with Long and Short Stitch (52). For caps of acorns make closely worked Bullion Stitches (8) going in all directions. Work Fly Stitches (41) very closely. (Numbers refer to stitches listed in Glossary, page 29.)

Finishing:
Finish cushion following instructions for Springtime Cushion (page 140).

Detail of Autumn Seat Cushion showing use of French Knots on goldenrod and Bullion Stitch on caps of acorns.

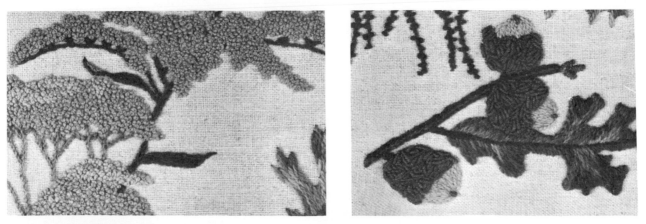

Diagram for Autumn Seat Cushion.

Color Key:
- A. Beige
- B. Golden Beige
- C. Apricot
- D. Pumpkin
- E. Yellow
- F. Gold
- G. Yellow Orange
- H. Light Golden Brown
- I. Dark Golden Brown
- J. Light Brown
- K. Medium Brown
- L. Dark Brown
- M. Bronze
- N. Light Green
- O. Medium Green
- P. Dark Green

⊢———Work narrow line

Numbers refer to stitches listed in glossary

Singapore Bird Chair Seat

Color photograph, following page 92

In this age of coordination it is fashionable to harmonize one's handbag with shoes, coat with dress, even towels with bed linen. What could be more appropriate than a set of dining chairs co-ordinated with one's treasured china? By this time you have developed the needlework skills to convert your china pattern into a beautiful design for a chair seat, or you can use the one shown here based on the Singapore Bird pattern of the Wedgwood Group.

[Chair Seat]

Size:
About 13" from front to back; about 14½" across front edge; about 11½" across back edge.

Materials:
¾ yard 36"-wide white linen
Crewel wool, one 30-yard card each: light blue, medium blue, light fern green, dark green, yellow, pink, rose and wine

Wedgwood china design which was adapted for embroidery.

Diagram for Singapore Bird Chair Seat.

Color Key:
A. Light Blue
B. Medium Blue
C. Light Fern Green
D. Dark Green
E. Yellow
F. Pink
G. Rose
H. Wine
⟋⟍——Work narrow line
Numbers refer to stitches listed in glossary

Detail of Singapore Bird Chair Seat.

14½″ x 13″ piece of 1″-thick foam rubber.
½ yard 36″-wide muslin
Staples

Pattern:
Enlarge diagram on page 145 (each small square = ½″ square). Make a paper pattern of your chair seat. Fit enlarged pattern into seat pattern. Make any adjustments of design necessary. Cut background fabric following seat pattern and allow 3″ extra on all edges. Transfer design to fabric.

Working Method:
Place work in an embroidery frame or hoop. Use one strand of wool throughout. Follow alphabetical key on diagram for colors. All leaves outside the center frame of the design are dark green Open Cretan Stitch (30). Flowers represented by small circles on the diagram are made up of four to six Lazy-Daisy Stitches (50). All dots are yellow French Knots (42) unless indicated otherwise. Large flower on the left alternates rows of rose and pink, starting at center with Straight Stitch (70) and alternating with rows of Blanket Stitch (5). (Numbers refer to stitches listed in Glossary, page 29.)

Finishing:
Follow directions for Covering a Removable Chair Seat (page 153).

Panel for Ecclesiastical Garment

Color photograph, following page 116

This inspiring chasuble was made for the minister of St. Albans Episcopal Church in Simsbury, Connecticut, by one of the church members. Reminiscent of the great Charter Oak which stands in nearby Hartford, it glorifies the passing days of the Trinity season from the tender greens of spring in the lower branches to the crown of snow on the treetop.

Although such a project is truly a labor of love, the technique is fairly simple and consists of an appliquéd tree trunk and little more than the Open Cretan Stitch for the leaves. Since the design is complete in itself, it would make a beautiful wall hanging for use anywhere.

[Panel]

Size:
Finished panel is 9" x 44½"

Materials:
For panel only: 1½ yards 36"-wide rayon, linen or heavy silk
For tree trunk: ⅜ yard 45"-wide brown wool fabric
Tweed knitting yarns in brown and olive shades
Brown sewing thread
6-strand cotton embroidery floss in brown, light yellow green, light gray green, apple green, medium green, olive, dark green, dark gray green, bottle green, peach, yellow, rust, brick, henna, scarlet and white. NOTE: A few shades can be pearl cotton rather than floss.

Pattern:
Enlarge diagram on page 149 for pattern (each small square = ½" square). Transfer design to background fabric cut 15" x 54". Using light-colored dressmaker's carbon paper, transfer design of the trunk to brown fabric. Cut out tree trunk allowing ¼" all around for hems.

Working Method:
Turn under hem allowances on tree trunk; baste. Place trunk in position on panel; baste and sew in place. Place work in a frame. Embroider tweed yarn down trunk, using Couching Stitch (27) held down with brown sewing thread and following vertical lines on pattern.

Work branches in close rows of brown Outline Stitch (53). Embroider earth around roots of tree in Running Stitch (58) in two strands of brown.

Embroider leaves in Open Cretan Stitch (30), using from three to six strands of floss and keeping the larger number of strands near the trunk of the tree. Each leaf should be worked in a single color and should be 1" to 1½" long. Start each leaf with small stitches at one end gradually increasing in size to about ½" across middle of leaf and tapering to small stitches at other end. Embroider leaves at bottom in light greens; work up to dark greens, then introduce the yellow, peach, then the reds. Soften the design by adding a few falling leaves at the sides in Fly Stitch (41). Work entire top in white Fly Stitch for the snow. Blend each color group with the one above and below. For example, work yellow and peach into the greens of late summer as well as up into the reds. See diagram and color photograph for details. (Numbers refer to stitches listed in Glossary, page 29.)

Finishing:
Trim panel to 12" x 47½". Turn under ½" allowance, then make 1" finished hems. Use a vestment you already have or make one from a pattern taken from an old one. The original panel was detachable so that the vestment could be washed regularly without the embroidery.

If you make this for a wall hanging, follow directions for Making a Wall Hanging (page 155).

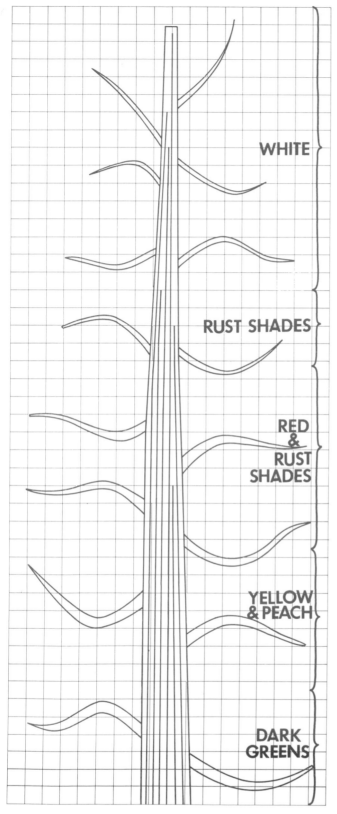

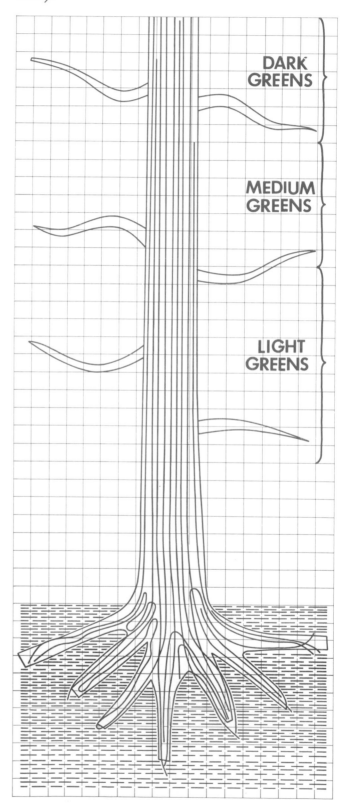

Below: *Diagram for Panel for Ecclesiastical Garment (lower section).*

WHITE

RUST SHADES

RED
&
RUST
SHADES

YELLOW
& PEACH

DARK
GREENS

DARK
GREENS

MEDIUM
GREENS

LIGHT
GREENS

Above: *Diagram for Panel for Ecclesiastical Garment (upper section).*

10. Professional Finishing Tips

You have just completed your embroidery. Now is the time to change it from a piece of fabric covered with stitchery into a beautiful piece of needlework that will always be a source of pride and satisfaction. Too many pieces of fine needlework are relegated to bottom drawers because the maker omits the finishing touches. As soon as the embroidery is finished, put your work into its final and complete form.

Be sure to sign and date your piece. Pencil in your name or initials and the year in a lower corner. Using only line stitches, work them for posterity. In fact, they don't have to be stuck in a corner; you might work your name right into the design.

WASHING OR DRY-CLEANING CREWEL

Perhaps your embroidery has become soiled with handling. It can be washed if you are sure that the background fabric is washable and that the colors of the yarns will not run. Just dip it in cool water and mild suds without twisting or squeezing. Rinse thoroughly, then let drip without squeezing. Roll in a towel until it is ready for blocking or pressing.

If the piece cannot be washed, freshen it with cleaning fluid or take it to a reputable dry cleaner.

BLOCKING

Blocking generally is a better method of finishing embroidery than pressing. If you have worked your embroidery in a frame, do not remove it. Dampen the embroidery, cover it with a damp cloth so that it dries slowly and allow the work to remain in the frame until dry.

If you have washed your embroidery or do not have it in a frame, block it as follows: Mark out on a board (perhaps a piece of plywood) the outside dimensions of your piece. While the work is wet, fasten the corners in place with rustproof thumbtacks or push pins. Then tack the center of each side. Now working from one side to the other, and top to bottom, tack halfway between places where work was just fastened until tacks are about ½" apart. Let dry.

PRESSING

When the work is not too wrinkled, sometimes only a light pressing rather than a complete blocking job is necessary. Pad your ironing board (or any large board) with terry towels. Use a steam iron or a dry iron and a damp press cloth. Place your embroidery wrong side up. Do not let the weight of the iron rest on the embroidery but steam press very lightly. Iron the rest of the piece according to the best method for the type of background fabric.

MAKING A PILLOW

Although ready-made pillow forms that will fit your pillow cover exactly can sometimes be purchased, it is usually necessary to make your own.

Flat, Knife-Edged Pillow

Cut two pieces of muslin to the pillow size desired allowing ½" seam allowance all around. If an unusual shape is needed, it is better to make a paper pattern first before cutting the muslin. Right sides together, stitch muslin pieces around edges, leaving center of one side open. Turn right side out. Stuff firmly, then slip-stitch the opening closed. A slip stitch is used for holding two folded edges together. Working from right to left, take a small stitch inside one fold; bring needle out. Take a similar stitch inside opposite fold. Continue across.

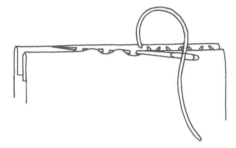

A number of stuffing materials may be found with the bedding supplies in a department store. Dacron® polyester and feathers are durable. Less expensive fillers are kapok, cotton batting and shredded foam.

Although a commercial pillow cover is usually made with a zipper, it is not necessary and the beginner is advised to omit it. Cut cover (embroidered piece) and backing piece the desired size plus ½″ seam allowance all around. Right sides together, stitch these two pieces together around edges, leaving center of one side open to insert pillow form. Trim seams. Turn right side out. Insert muslin pillow form. Fold in raw edges. Slip-stitch closed (see instructions for slip stitching above). This stitching can be removed easily when the cover needs washing or cleaning.

If a cording effect is desired (as on the Ascension Balloon Pillow, page 108), a twisted cord, available from the upholstery trimming department, can be tacked all around the seam of the pillow.

Box Pillow

Cut two pieces of muslin to the size pillow desired plus ½″ seam allowance all around. Cut a muslin boxing strip 2″ wide (or width desired; includes ½″ seam allowance on each edge) and long enough to fit around pillow plus 1″. Right sides together, baste and stitch muslin boxing strip around one piece of muslin. Seam together narrow ends of boxing strip. Baste and stitch other piece of muslin to boxing strip, leaving center of one side open. Trim Seams. Turn right side out. Fill muslin pillow firmly. Fold in raw edges and slip-stitch opening closed (see page 152).

Cut pillow top (embroidered piece) and back piece to desired size plus ½″ seam allowances all around. Cut boxing strip of same fabric as embroidered piece and same size as muslin boxing strip. Cover cording (with fabric strips cut on the bias). Make long enough to go around the top piece and the back piece of the pillow. Baste cording around the right sides of top piece and the back piece, raw edges facing out. Finish as for muslin pillow. Insert muslin pillow into embroidered pillow. Fold in raw edges and slip-stitch opening closed (see page 152).

COVERING A REMOVABLE CHAIR SEAT

Chairs differ greatly in construction so you will have to upholster the seat according to the best method for your chair. If you have a simple slip seat, remove it from the chair. Remove old upholstery fabric. Replace the padding if necessary, following method used for old padding. Re-cover with new muslin, stapling or tacking it smoothly in place. Center embroidered piece on seat; hold with pins. Cut off excess fabric, allowing enough to turn under edges. Turn edges to underside of seat. Staple or tack in place. Replace seat in chair.

FRAMING A PICTURE

Having needlework framed professionally can be quite expensive, and many professional framers are not experienced in handling needlework. With a little care and experience you can do a better job yourself. Since frames can be expensive, be on the lookout for nice ones in thrift shops and antique shops. It's amazing what a little paint or dark shoe polish can do to restore a frame. Or you can use the outer ring of a plain round or oval embroidery hoop as a frame and tape the mounted embroidery in place on a cardboard backing.

It is wise to have the appropriate frame before you begin a piece of needlework. First remove the nails and hooks on the back. Clean or refinish the frame if necessary. Cut a piece of heavy cardboard to fit the opening on the back of the frame—but be sure that it isn't too tight a fit.

Here's a tip just for needleworkers who prefer not to us glass in their frames. With scissors, cut a piece of ¼"-thick foam rubber the same size as the cardboard. Glue or cement it to the cardboard. This will make the stitches stand up and give a nice cushioned effect to your embroidery.

Trim embroidery so that it is 1½" to 2" larger all around than cardboard. Place foam rubber side of cardboard on back of embroidery, lining up the grain of the fabric with the edges of the cardboard. Temporarily hold the embroidery in place with a few straight pins stuck in the edges of cardboard. At the top and bottom of picture, fold the extra fabric to the back and fasten with a strip of masking tape. Repeat the process with the extra fabric on each side. If the corners are too thick, it may be necessary to trim away the lower layer of the folds and retape the fabric in place.

Whether or not you use glass in your frame is a matter of personal preference. Many needleworkers feel that glass flattens their work, others feel that it keeps it clean. If you do use glass, this is the time to insert it in the frame. Now put picture face down in frame. Hold in place with fine wire nails hammered into the center of each side and top and bottom of frame. If it's a very large picture, one or two more nails may be required on each side.

When you use glass, you may want a dust cover on the back. First apply a thin line of glue all around near the edge of the back of the frame. Lay a sheet of brown paper on it. When dry, cut away excess paper.

Insert hooks and attach picture wire.

A picture framed without glass may show soil after it has been hanging for a while. If it does, remove from the frame, wash and block it, or dry-clean it as described on page 150. Then replace it in the frame and hold it in place again with fine wire nails hammered in center of top and bottom and center of each side.

MAKING A WALL PANEL

Many pictures are more attractive unframed. To mount them, cut backing from heavy cardboard, thin plywood or other type of composition board available at lumberyards. Mount the embroidery on the backing following directions for Framing a Picture (page 153). If you are using plywood or composition board, you may prefer to staple your embroidery in place rather than tape it. Attach an adhesive cloth picture hanger on cardboard; use picture wire on plywood.

MAKING A WALL HANGING

Wall Hanging with Casing

Cut your embroidered piece to desired size plus at least 1" hem allowance on each side and lower edge, 1½" allowance on top edge. For larger hangings, leave wider allowances. Hem sides, then the lower edge, either by machine or hand. Make top hem, leaving the ends open. Insert a dowel or curtain rod of the proper length in casing formed by top hem. To hang, support dowel on a nail at each end or tie a decorative cord on the ends of the dowel. NOTE: Wall hanging may need dressmaker's weights sewed to lower edge to keep it even. Or a dowel can be inserted in lower hem for the same purpose.

Wall Hanging with Tabs

A more formal type of hanging can be made as follows: Cut embroidered piece to desired size plus ½" hem allowance all around. Cut a piece of lining material same size. Right sides together, stitch sides and lower edge. Clip corners. Turn and press. Turn the top hem allowance on the hanging and on the lining to the inside; press (do not stitch).

For tabs, cut a strip 2½" wide, 12" long. Fold strip in half lengthwise, with the right side inside. Stitch along raw edge with ¼" seam. Turn and press. Cut strip into four tabs 3" long. NOTE: You may need more tabs for a large hanging. Fold tabs in half crosswise and insert raw ends in top of wall hanging between hanging and lining. Space them evenly. Slip-stitch (page 152) or machine-stitch opening closed. Insert dowel or curtain rod in tabs.

HOW TO MAKE COASTERS

Apply glue to a cardboard square the size of the finished coaster. When tacky, fasten embroidery to it. Trim edges to fit cardboard. Cut ⅛"-wide cardboard strips the length of each side. Glue strips on top of edges of embroidered piece. Paint cardboard with ink or watercolors to match background of embroidery. Place glass on coaster (on top of cardboard strips). Bind in place with tape cut the length of each side. Cut ends of tape diagonally to form neat mitered corners.

HOW TO MAKE A TOTE BAG

Cut embroidered piece and back of bag to size desired, plus ½" seam allowance all around. Cut two interfacing pieces same size as front and back of bag. Baste an interfacing piece to the wrong side of each of these pieces. Right sides together, stitch these two pieces around three sides with ½" seams. Trim seams; turn right side out; press. Turn under ½" on top edge; press.

For lining, cut two pieces same size as front and back of bag. Stitch exactly as you did the bag, making lining a fraction of an inch smaller all around and omitting interfacings. Do not turn.

For handles, cut two strips each 2½" wide and the length desired, plus 1". Fold each strip in thirds lengthwise. Turn under raw edge and sew in place. Or attach ready-made handles (available in needle-work shops) when bag is completed.

Slip lining into bag. Insert ends of handles between bag and lining. Tack firmly in place. Slip-stitch lining to bag along top edge (see page 152).

HOW TO MAKE A HANDBAG

Cut out handbag shapes, leaving ½" seam allowance all around.

Cut two similar pieces of interfacing and two of lining fabric. Baste an interfacing piece to wrong side of each bag piece. Right sides together, stitch bottom and sides of bag up to points where it joins frame. Trim and clip seams. Turn and press carefully. Turn under and baste raw edges. Sew bag to frame.

Stitch lining pieces together as for bag, making lining a bare fraction of an inch smaller than the bag. Do not turn. Trim and clip seams. Turn under and baste raw edges. Tack inside bag.

101 Things You Can Decorate

(On items to be washed, use colorfast cotton thread.)

Address Book Cover	Covers for Director's Chair
Afghan	Credit Cards Case
Album Cover	Cummerbund
Apron	Cushions
Bed Canopy	Desk Accessories
Bed (or Wall) Caddy	Dog Coat
Bedspread	Doll's Dress
Bell Pull	Draperies
Belt	Dress
Blouse or Shirt	Earrings
Book Bag	Evening Coat
Book Cover	Eyeglass Case
Bookends	Family Tree
Bookmark	Footstool
Bulletin Board Frame	Greeting Card
Buttons	Guest Towels
Cafe Curtains	Guitar Strap
Carriage Cover	Handkerchief Case
Checkbook Cover	Handkerchiefs
Child's Growth Chart	Hassock
Christmas Tree Skirt	Hatband
Clock Face	Headband
Coasters	Herb Chart
Collar	Jacket
Cosmetic Case	Jeans (dungarees)

With Crewel Stitches

Jewelry Box Top — Seat Cushion

Jewelry Case — Seat Pad

Knitting Bag — Sewing Case

Lap Robe — Shawl

Lingerie Case — Shoulder Bag

Marriage Record Frame — Skirt

Mat for Picture Frame — Slacks

Mirror Frame — Stole

Mittens — Stuffed Animal

Music Box Top — Sweater

Napkin Ring — Table Cover

Napkins — Table Mats

Pennant — Table Top (under glass)

Perpetual Calendar Frame — Telephone Book Cover

Piano Bench Seat — Tennis Racket Cover

Picture — Tie-backs

Picture Frame — Tote Bag

Pin or Brooch — Tray (under glass)

Plaque — Toaster Cover

Pocket (of skirt, dress) — TV Weekly Program Cover

Poncho — Upholstery

Purse — Vest

Purse Accessories — Wall Hanging

Head Scarf — Watch Strap

Screen — Writing Case

Yardstick Holder

Credits

The projects described and photographed in this book were designed and embroidered by the needleworkers whose names are listed below:

Peacock (page 10), designed and embroidered by Dorothy Mattick of Loughton, Essex. Student of Joan Edwards, Royal School of Needlework, London.

Chessmen (page 10), designed and embroidered by Phyllis R. Price of London. Student of Joan Edwards, Royal School of Needlework, London.

St. Michael (page 21), designed and embroidered by Alexander W. Fraser of Folkestone, Kent. Student of Joan Edwards, Royal School of Needlework, London.

Song of the Sea Sampler (page 77), designed and embroidered by the author.

Twining Vine Bookmark (page 80), designed and embroidered by the author.

Decorative Mirror (following page 92), designed and embroidered by Solweig Hedin of New York City.

Butterfly and Bird Designs (following page 92), designed and embroidered by Sharon Perch of New York City.

Whirling Wheels Pillow (following page 92), designed and embroidered by Solweig Hedin of New York City.

Winter Wonderland (page 94), designed and embroidered by Charles Barnes and David P. Blake of New York City.

Accent Crewel (page 97), embroidered by the author.

Classic Tote Bag (following page 92), designed and embroidered by Solweig Hedin of New York City.

Paisley Pillow (following page 92), designed and embroidered by Charles Barnes and David P. Blake of New York City.

Fanciful Fish Picture (following page 116), designed by Michael Cannarozzi of White Plains, New York. Embroidered by Carmela Cannarozzi.

Abstract Picture (following page 116), designed and embroidered by the author.

Ascension Balloon Pillow (following page 92), designed and embroidered by the author.

Bird and Tulip Pillow (following page 92), designed and embroidered by Solweig Hedin of New York City.

Calico Cat Cushion (following page 92), designed by Virginia Zito of Irvington, New York. Embroidered by Betty Celic Holden of Simsbury, Connecticut.

Zinnias and Asters Picture (adapted for cover design and following page 116), designed and embroidered by the author.

Antique Floral Pillow (following page 92), adapted and embroidered by the author.

Medusa Head Picture (page 125), designed by the author. Embroidered by Frank L. Kitchen of Craigville, New York.

Summer Handbag (following page 92), designed by the author. Embroidered by Bertha Boehm of Chicago, Illinois.

Graphic Wall Hanging (following page 92), designed by the author. Embroidered by Bertha Boehm of Chicago, Illinois.

Proud Rooster Picture (following page 116), adapted by William Blume of New York City. Embroidered by Frank L. Kitchen of Craigville, New York.

Garden of Flowers Picture (following page 116), designed and embroidered by June Beveridge of Simsbury, Connecticut.

Seat Cushions (following page 116), designed by Joan Woodham of Westport, Connecticut and Doris Boas of Wilton, Connecticut. Embroidered by Doris Boas.

Singapore Bird Chair Seat (following page 92), adapted and embroidered by Betty Celic Holden of Simsbury, Connecticut.

Panel for Ecclesiastical Garment (following page 116), designed and embroidered by Jane Bannister of West Simsbury, Connecticut.

Index